P9-DHK-551

FIRST BLOOD
Fort Sumter to Bull Run

NEW FAIRFIELD FREE PUBLIC
LIBRARY
NEW FAIRFIELD,CT.

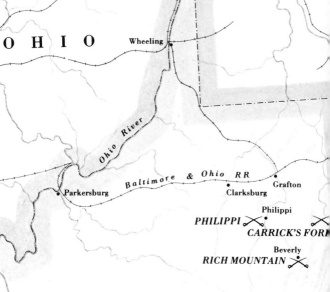

THE EASTERN THEATER, APRIL–JULY 1861

In the three months following the Confederate capture of Fort Sumter, developments in the Eastern Theater were powerfully shaped by the railroads. While Union and Confederate forces fought minor engagements (*crossed swords*) at Big Bethel and in western Virginia, more than 30,000 soldiers on each side were sent by rail to northern Virginia via Richmond or Washington. The Confederates, bracing to repulse a Union invasion, manned a line along Bull Run, where they could be reinforced by rail-borne units sent to Manassas Junction from Richmond and the Shenandoah Valley. On July 21, 1861, the first big battle of the Civil War was joined at Bull Run.

OHIO

Pittsburgh

Wheeling

Ohio River

Baltimore & Ohio RR

Parkersburg

Clarksburg

Grafton

Philippi

PHILIPPI

CARRICK'S FORD

Beverly

RICH MOUNTAIN

Charleston

Kanawha River

Greenbrier River

Lexington

KENTUCKY

Virginia & Tennessee RR

TENNESSEE

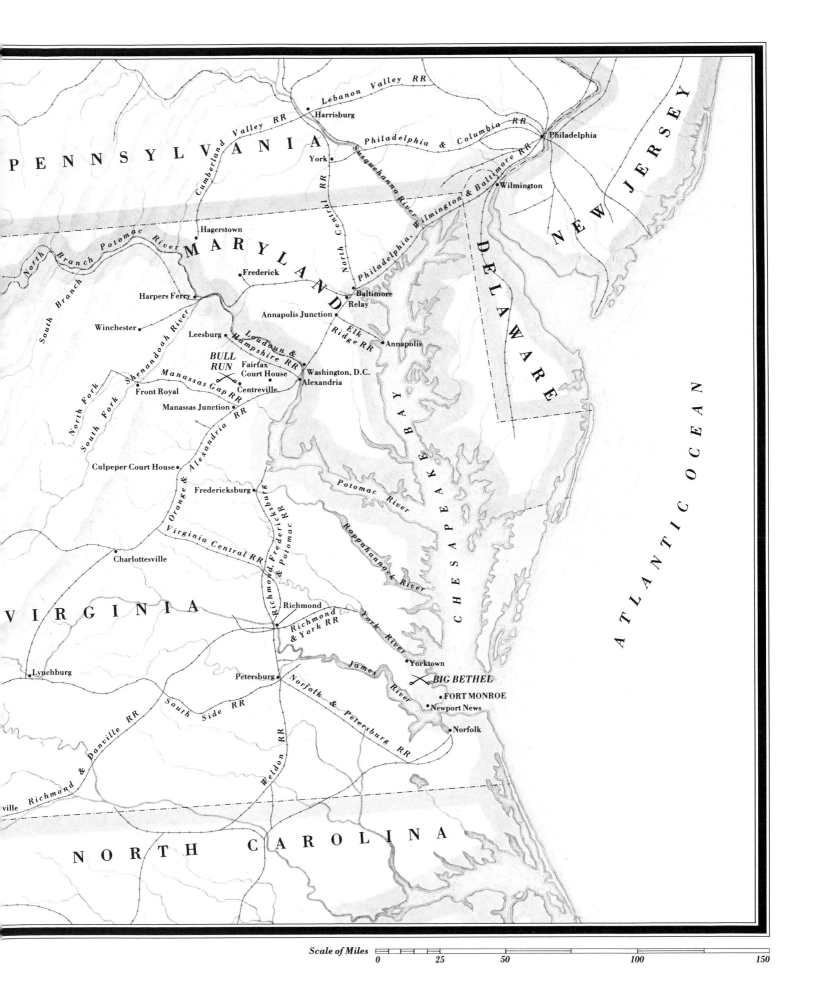

PENNSYLVANIA

NEW JERSEY

Lebanon Valley RR

Harrisburg

Philadelphia & Columbia RR

Philadelphia

Cumberland Valley RR

York

North Central RR

Susquehanna River

Wilmington

DELAWARE

North Branch Potomac River

Hagerstown

MARYLAND

South Branch

Frederick

Philadelphia, Wilmington & Baltimore RR

Harpers Ferry

Baltimore

Relay

Winchester

Shenandoah River

Annapolis Junction

Elk Ridge RR

Annapolis

Leesburg

Loudoun & Hampshire RR

BULL
RUN

Fairfax
Court House

Washington, D.C.

Centreville

Alexandria

North Fork

South Fork

Manassas Gap RR

Front Royal

Manassas Junction

& Alexandria RR

CHESAPEAKE BAY

ATLANTIC OCEAN

Culpeper Court House

Orange & Alexandria RR

Fredericksburg

Richmond, Fredericksburg & Potomac RR

Virginia Central RR

Potomac River

Charlottesville

Rappahannock River

VIRGINIA

Richmond

Richmond & York RR

York River

Yorktown

Lynchburg

James River

BIG BETHEL

Petersburg

Norfolk & Petersburg RR

FORT MONROE

South Side RR

Newport News

Richmond & Danville RR

Weldon RR

Norfolk

ville *Richmond &*

NORTH CAROLINA

Scale of Miles

0   25   50   100   150

Other Publications:

THE TIME-LIFE GARDENER'S GUIDE
MYSTERIES OF THE UNKNOWN
TIME FRAME
FIX IT YOURSELF
FITNESS, HEALTH & NUTRITION
SUCCESSFUL PARENTING
HEALTHY HOME COOKING
UNDERSTANDING COMPUTERS
LIBRARY OF NATIONS
THE ENCHANTED WORLD
THE KODAK LIBRARY OF CREATIVE PHOTOGRAPHY
GREAT MEALS IN MINUTES
PLANET EARTH
COLLECTOR'S LIBRARY OF THE CIVIL WAR
THE EPIC OF FLIGHT
THE GOOD COOK
WORLD WAR II
HOME REPAIR AND IMPROVEMENT
THE OLD WEST

For information on and a full description of any of the
Time-Life Books series listed above, please call 1-800-621-
7026 or write:
Reader Information
Time-Life Customer Service
P.O. Box C-32068
Richmond, Virginia 23261-2068

This volume is one of a series that chronicles in full the
events of the American Civil War, 1861-1865.
Other books in the series include:

Brother against Brother: The War Begins
The Blockade: Runners and Raiders
The Road to Shiloh: Early Battles in the West
Forward to Richmond: McClellan's Peninsular Campaign
Decoying the Yanks: Jackson's Valley Campaign
Confederate Ordeal: The Southern Home Front
Lee Takes Command: From Seven Days to Second Bull Run
The Coastal War: Chesapeake Bay to Rio Grande
Tenting Tonight: The Soldier's Life
The Bloodiest Day: The Battle of Antietam
War on the Mississippi: Grant's Vicksburg Campaign
Rebels Resurgent: Fredericksburg to Chancellorsville
Twenty Million Yankees: The Northern Home Front
Gettysburg: The Confederate High Tide
The Struggle for Tennessee: Tupelo to Stones River
The Fight for Chattanooga: Chickamauga to Missionary Ridge
Spies, Scouts and Raiders: Irregular Operations
The Battles for Atlanta: Sherman Moves East
The Killing Ground: Wilderness to Cold Harbor
Sherman's March: Atlanta to the Sea
Death in the Trenches: Grant at Petersburg
War on the Frontier: The Trans-Mississippi West
The Shenandoah in Flames: The Valley Campaign of 1864
Pursuit to Appomattox: The Last Battles
The Assassination: The Death of the President
The Nation Reunited: War's Aftermath
Master Index: An Illustrated Guide

The Cover: Confederate cavalrymen *(right)* under
Colonel J.E.B. Stuart attack the gaudily uniformed
11th New York Fire Zouaves during the Battle of
Bull Run on July 21, 1861. In the foreground, Union
troops wearing white havelocks to shield their necks
from the sun fire a volley at the enemy horsemen.

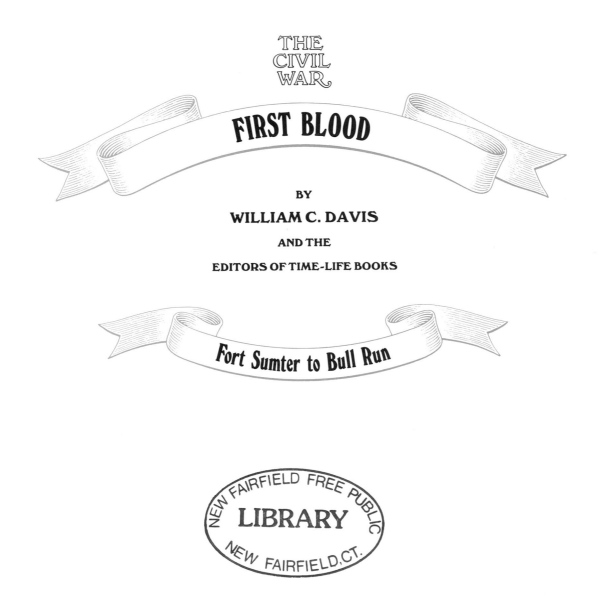

THE
CIVIL
WAR

FIRST BLOOD

BY

WILLIAM C. DAVIS

AND THE

EDITORS OF TIME-LIFE BOOKS

Fort Sumter to Bull Run

NEW FAIRFIELD FREE PUBLIC
LIBRARY
NEW FAIRFIELD, CT.

TIME-LIFE BOOKS, ALEXANDRIA, VIRGINIA

Time-Life Books Inc.
is a wholly owned subsidiary of

TIME INCORPORATED

FOUNDER: Henry R. Luce 1898-1967

Editor-in-Chief: Henry Anatole Grunwald
President: J. Richard Munro
Chairman of the Board: Ralph P. Davidson
Corporate Editor: Jason McManus
Group Vice President, Books: Reginald K. Brack Jr.
Vice President, Books: George Artandi

TIME-LIFE BOOKS INC.

EDITOR: George Constable
Executive Editor: George Daniels
Editorial General Manager: Neal Goff
Director of Design: Louis Klein
Editorial Board: Dale M. Brown, Roberta Conlan,
Ellen Phillips, Gerry Schremp, Gerald Simons,
Rosalind Stubenberg, Kit van Tulleken
Director of Research: Phyllis K. Wise
Director of Photography: John Conrad Weiser

PRESIDENT: William J. Henry
Senior Vice President: Christopher T. Linen
Vice Presidents: Stephen L. Bair, Robert A. Ellis,
John M. Fahey Jr., Juanita T. James, James L. Mercer,
Joanne A. Pello, Paul R. Stewart, Christian Strasser

The Civil War
Editor: Gerald Simons
Deputy Editor: Henry Woodhead
Designer: Herbert H. Quarmby
Chief Researchers: Jane Edwin, Philip Brandt George

Editorial Staff for *First Blood*
Associate Editors: David S. Thomson (text);
Richard Kenin (pictures)
Staff Writers: Adrienne George, John Newton,
Kirk Y. Saunders
Researchers: Susan Kelly, Brian C. Pohanka (principals);
Harris J. Andrews, Kristin Baker, Feroline P. Burrage,
Jayne Wise
Assistant Designers: Jeanne Potter,
Cynthia T. Richardson
Copy Coordinator: Allan Fallow
Picture Coordinator: Eric Godwin
Editorial Assistant: Annette T. Wilkerson

Editorial Operations
Design: Ellen Robling (assistant director)
Copy Room: Diane Ullius
Production: Celia Beattie
Quality Control: James J. Cox (director), Sally Collins
Library: Louise D. Forstall

Correspondents: Elisabeth Kraemer-Singh (Bonn);
Margot Hapgood, Dorothy Bacon (London); Miriam
Hsia, Lucy T. Voulgaris (New York); Maria Vincenza
Aloisi, Josephine du Brusle (Paris); Ann Natanson
(Rome). Valuable assistance was also provided by:
Gail Cameron Wescott (Atlanta); Cheryl Crooks
(Los Angeles); Lynne Bachleda (Nashville); Carolyn
Chubet (New York).

The Author:
William C. Davis was for 13 years editor of the *Civil War Times Illustrated* and is the author or editor of more than a dozen books on the Civil War, among them *Brother against Brother* in the Time-Life Books Civil War series, *Battle at Bull Run, The Orphan Brigade* and *The Deep Waters of the Proud,* the first in a three-volume narrative of the War. He is also editor of the six-volume photographic history of the conflict, *The Image of War: 1861-1865.*

The Consultants:
Colonel John R. Elting, USA (Ret.), a former Associate Professor at West Point, is the author of *Battles for Scandinavia* in the Time-Life Books World War II series and *The Battle of Bunker's Hill, The Battles of Saratoga, Military History and Atlas of the Napoleonic Wars* and *American Army Life.* He is also editor of the three volumes of *Military Uniforms in America, 1755-1867,* and associate editor of *The West Point Atlas of American Wars.*

James I. Robertson Jr. is C. P. Miles Professor of History at Virginia Tech. The recipient of the Nevins-Freeman Award and other prizes in the field of Civil War history, he has written or edited some 20 books, which include *The Stonewall Brigade, Civil War Books: A Critical Bibliography* and *Civil War Sites in Virginia.*

William A. Frassanito, a Civil War historian and lecturer specializing in photograph analysis, is the author of two award-winning studies, *Gettysburg: A Journey in Time* and *Antietam: The Photographic Legacy of America's Bloodiest Day,* and a companion volume, *Grant and Lee, The Virginia Campaigns.* He has also served as chief consultant to the photographic history series *The Image of War.*

Les Jensen, Director of the Second Armored Division Museum at Fort Hood, Texas, specializes in Civil War artifacts and is a conservator of historic flags. He is a contributor to *The Image of War* series, a freelance writer and consultant for numerous Civil War publications and museums, and a member of the Company of Military Historians. He was formerly Curator of the Museum of the Confederacy in Richmond, Virginia, and of the U.S. Army Transportation Museum at Fort Eustis, Virginia.

Michael McAfee specializes in military uniforms and has been Curator of Uniforms and History at the West Point Museum since 1970. A fellow of the Company of Military Historians, he coedited with Colonel John Elting *Long Endure: The Civil War Years,* and he collaborated with Frederick Todd on *American Military Equipage, 1851-1872.* He has written numerous articles for *Military Images Magazine* as well as *Artillery of the American Revolution, 1775-1783.*

©1983 Time-Life Books Inc. All rights reserved.
No part of this book may be reproduced in any form
or by any electronic or mechanical means, including
information storage and retrieval devices or systems,
without prior written permission from the publisher,
except that brief passages may be quoted for reviews
Fifth printing. Revised 1988. Printed in U.S.A.
Published simultaneously in Canada.
School and library distribution by Silver Burdett
Company, Morristown, New Jersey 07960.

TIME-LIFE is a trademark of Time Incorporated U.S.A.

Library of Congress Cataloguing in Publication Data
Davis, William C., 1946-
    First blood.
    (Civil War series; v. 2)
    Bibliography: p.
    Includes index.
    1. United States — History — Civil War, 1861-1865 —
Campaigns. I. Time-Life Books. II. Title. III. Series.
E470.D37 1983   973.7'3   82-19546
ISBN 0-8094-4704-5 (retail ed.)
ISBN 0-8094-4705-3 (lib. bdg.)

NEW FAIRFIELD FREE PUBLIC
LIBRARY
NEW FAIRFIELD, CT.

CONTENTS

Patriotic Northern volunteers, galvanized by the Confederate shelling of Fort Sumter (*center*), rush to defend the Union in this allegorical

painting. The artist completed the Capitol's new dome, still under construction at the start of the War, to suggest the country's might.

The Shadow War

*"War! An arm'd race is advancing! The welcome for battle,
no turning away; War! Be it weeks, months, or years, an arm'd
race is advancing to welcome it."*

WALT WHITMAN

1

Journalist William Howard Russell, touring the American South for *The Times* of London, chanced to be in Goldsboro, North Carolina, on April 15, 1861, just after word arrived by telegraph that Fort Sumter had surrendered to Confederate troops. The reserved Englishman was taken aback by the frantic celebration that erupted all around him. It was a carnival of "flushed faces, wild eyes, screaming mouths hurrahing for 'Jeff Davis' and 'the Southern Confederacy,' so that the yells overpowered the discordant bands which were busy with 'Dixie's Land.'" Though North Carolina was one of the four Southern states that had not yet seceded, Russell concluded that it would not long remain in the Union: "Here was the true revolutionary furor in full sway."

The North reacted to Sumter's fall with hardly less emotion, though obviously with less joy. The 20 million Northerners were stunned, frightened and above all outraged by the attack on the American flag. An angry mob of New Yorkers stormed the offices of the pro-Southern New York *Herald* and, under threat of burning everything in sight, forced publisher James Gordon Bennett to display the Stars and Stripes. In Boston, bells tolled all day long. In Milwaukee, a judge and jury walked out of the courtroom to enlist as a group, with the judge as captain.

From both sides came vindictive demands and loud blasts of bravado. To ensure proper punishment for the treasonous Southern rebels, *The New York Times* wanted to "carry terror into the hearts of the Confederates," and also "to conquer them—not merely to defeat but to conquer, to subjugate them!" Replying in kind from the temporary capital of the Confederacy at Montgomery, Alabama, Secretary of War Leroy Pope Walker promised an admiring crowd that their new nation's flag "will, before the 1st of May, float over the dome of the old Capitol in Washington."

And so, at long last, the waiting was over. For fully five decades, the problems of states' rights and slavery had stirred mounting sectional hostility. Americans were a people who prided themselves on their pragmatism, and they had labored earnestly, often cleverly, to reconcile the clashing interests and traditions of North and South. But in the end they had failed. Reason and compromise had failed, and now, to the great relief of many people on both sides, the solution was left to the soldiery. The War had finally come.

Or had it? The two most powerful Americans, Abraham Lincoln and Jefferson Davis, made public statements indicating that they were not quite convinced. On hearing of the fall of Sumter, Davis said, "Separation is not, of necessity, final." Said Lincoln: "I have desired as sincerely as any man— I sometimes think more than any man—that our present difficulties might be settled. I will not say that all hope is yet gone."

Davis, that grim-faced, unbending man, was cautiously hopeful, because what he wanted from the North could be granted merely by default. "All we ask," he said, "is to be left alone." Davis firmly believed that the Southern states had the Constitutional right to secede from the Union and were now an independent combination of sovereign states. Should the federal government choose to dispute his logic and impose its will by force of arms, Davis would be prepared: In March he had issued a call for 100,000 Southern volunteers, and privately he feared that they would all be needed. But if Lincoln chose not to contest the Confederacy's right to an independent existence, Davis and his government would, in due course, consider peaceable trade with the United States.

Ultimately, Davis and the South based their hope for peace on an error in judgment. Like so many Southerners devoted to the ideal of states' rights, the President of the Confederacy could not grasp the strength of feeling that Northerners held for their national union or the depth of their fear that secession would strike a death blow to the American republic and the democratic experiment. Davis therefore could not quite believe that Northern men in the hundreds of thousands would actually fight for national union, abolition and the other principles they proclaimed to the skies. So he was content to sit back and wait, taking no aggressive military action unless the North invaded Southern territory.

Lincoln's position was much more difficult. Believing the United States to be an indissoluble unit, he maintained that the seven states of the Deep South that had thus far announced secession were in fact still part of the Union and merely engaged in a misguided rebellion. Having often pledged himself to preserve the Union, the President was automatically committed to quashing the insurrection. Unless Davis' government conceded the error of its ways, the United States would have to assume the unattractive role of aggressor.

Lincoln faced other sobering choices. In mid-April the United States Congress would adjourn. This situation would permit him to put emergency measures into effect without an embarrassing clash with Congress over the proper executive and legislative authority in the matter. If Lincoln was correct in his opinion that the South was in a state of insurrection, he had authority to take police action under the Militia Act of 1792, as amended in 1795; but if the Constitution's reference to the states as "sovereign" entities was taken literally, then, as Jefferson Davis alleged, the Southern states indeed had a right to secede from the Union. And if the Confederacy was therefore a nation at war with the United States, Lincoln would, by resorting to force, usurp Congress' exclusive right to declare war.

Yet for all practical purposes, it took only bloodshed to make a war, even if the contest was legally a mere rebellion. It was largely because so little blood had been shed thus far that both Presidents held out hope that war by any name might still be avoided. Curiously, neither the Federal garrison at Sumter nor the Confederate troops surrounding it had killed a single enemy soldier during their 33-hour cannon duel. And historic precedents argued that until men had died for their cause in ample number, peace might always be snatched from the jaws of war.

No one in mid-April of 1861 could guess whether or when enough blood would be spilled to seal the two countries' commitment to wage war. Indeed most people on

Engulfed by patriotic spectators, civic and military officials in Detroit swear an oath of allegiance to the United States just after the attack on Fort Sumter. As part of Detroit's "loyalty demonstration," 3,000 children were hustled to the City Hall to sing "The Star-Spangled Banner."

both sides felt certain that a single, gallant, nearly bloodless battle would resolve the issue neatly and almost at once. They were romantics all, and all would be disillusioned. Three nerve-racking months of suspense would produce no decision; this was a period of shadow war, a time of confusion and preparation and ferocious rhetoric. Finally, in the heat of July in northern Virginia, beside a sluggish stream with the homely name of Bull Run, two inept armies would blunder into a shocking battle that guaranteed the real war—and a protracted and tragically costly one at that.

Jefferson Davis did not have to wait long for a clear sign of Northern intentions. On April 15, Lincoln forged the first link in the chain of events that led to Bull Run. Being a tough-minded politician, he seized the opportunity to act without Congressional encumbrance and issued a strong proclamation. Because the seven seceded Southern states had opposed and obstructed the laws of the United States, and because they had "constituted combinations too powerful to be suppressed by the ordinary course of judicial proceedings," he called forth 75,000 militiamen to serve for three months "in order to suppress said combinations and cause the laws to be duly executed."

Lincoln then appealed to all loyal citizens "to favor, facilitate and aid in this effort to maintain the honor, the integrity, and the existence of our National Union, and the perpetuity of popular government, and to redress wrongs already long enough endured." He gave the existing Southern military forces 20 days to disband and disperse. The implication was that if they did so, all would be forgiven, and that if they did not, his intention to "redress wrongs" would be fulfilled. At the end of his proclamation, Lincoln summoned Congress to convene in special session, although not until the Fourth of July—not until public opinion had time to solidify behind him, as he felt sure it would. And five days later, the President imposed a naval blockade on all Southern ports.

These bold moves excited great enthusiasm throughout the North. In every city and country town, young men turned out to enlist in huge numbers (pages 32-43), and every state quickly exceeded the quota of regiments that Lincoln had asked the governors to raise. Republicans and other Lincoln backers, who had suffered through four years of vacillation during the Democratic administration of James Buchanan, let go a loud collective sigh of pride and relief. Lincoln was backed by Buchanan himself, and by Lincoln's recent rival for the presidency, Stephen A. Douglas, who ruined his health traveling the country speaking for national solidarity. Lincoln even won the endorsement of radical abolitionists in Boston, men and women who had burned copies of the Constitution and disowned the Union because both the document and the government had so long tolerated slavery. Said abolitionist leader Wendell Phillips at a war rally in Boston's Music Hall, "For the first time in my antislavery life I speak under the Stars and Stripes."

Now it was the Southerners' turn to be outraged. Jefferson Davis bridled at the naked threat of Lincoln's call to arms and abandoned his last flickering hope for peace. Southerners of every degree gave vent to their long-festering rage at the abolitionists, the federal government and the Northern financiers, who had allegedly exploited the

13

South like a backward colony for decades. The Confederate enlistment drive, which had been bubbling along satisfactorily since March, boiled over. Young men all across the South stormed the recruiting offices, eager to risk their lives to repel the threatened invasion by the despised Yankees. The defense of the Southern homeland shortly took on mystical dimensions.

Unable to perceive that the South's own acts had provoked Lincoln's strong measures, many hotbloods were carried away by dreams of battlefield glory. "So impatient did I become for starting," recalled one Southern recruit, "that I felt like ten thousand pins were pricking me in every part of my body." In every courthouse town across the Confederacy, soldiers enlisted in companies and chose their officers, often after spirited election campaigns. Then they drilled in the town square and set off for local assembly points to be organized into regiments. They went full of hopes, waving flags made by their sweethearts and shouting the marvelous boastful names of their companies. Here came the Tallapoosa Thrashers, the Cherokee Lincoln Killers and the Barbour County Yankee Hunters.

They were romantics, young and spirited, lured by adventure, goaded by patriotism to flights of operatic passion. Charles C. Jones, a Georgia boy in a volunteer company in Savannah, wrote his parents in exaggerated dudgeon: "Can you imagine a more suicidal, outrageous, and exasperating policy than that inaugurated by the fanatical administration at Washington? Heaven forbid that they ever attempt to set foot upon this land of sunshine, of high-souled honor and of liberty. It puzzles the imagination to conceive the stupidity, the fanaticism and the unmitigat-

Head Quarters, Virginia Forces,
STAUNTON, VA.

MEN OF VIRGINIA, TO THE RESCUE !

Your soil has been invaded by your Abolition foes, and we call upon you to rally at once, and drive them back. We want Volunteers to march immediately to Grafton and report for duty. Come one ! Come ALL ! and render the service due to your State and Country. Fly to arms, and succour your brave brothers who are now in the field.

The Volunteers from the Counties of Pendleton, Highland, Bath, Alleghany, Monroe, Mercer, and other Counties convenient to that point, will immediately organize, and report at Monterey, in Highland County, where they will join the Companies from the Valley, marching on Grafton. The Volunteers from the Counties of Hardy, Hampshire, Randolph, Pocahontas, Greenbrier, and other Counties convenient, will in like manner report at Beverly. And the Volunteers from the Counties of Upshur, Lewis, Barbour, and other Counties, will report at Philippi, in Barbour County. The Volunteers, as soon as they report at the above points, will be furnished with arms, saddle, &c., &c.

Action ! Action ! should be our rallying motto, and the sentiment of Virginia's inspired Orator, "Give me Liberty or give me Death," animate every loyal son of the Old Dominion ! Let us drive back the invading foot of a brutal and desperate foe, or leave a record to posterity that we died bravely defending our homes and firesides,—the honor of our wives and daughters,—and the sacred graves of our ancestors !

[Done by Authority.]
M. G. HARMAN, Maj. Commd'g
at Staunton.
J. M. HECK, Lt. Col. Va. Vol.
R. E. COWAN, Maj. Va. Vol.
May 30, 1861.

A Virginia broadside, published shortly after Union forces invaded the state in late May of 1861, appeals urgently for volunteers to defend "our homes and firesides,—the honor of our wives and daughters,—and the sacred graves of our ancestors!"

ed rascality which impel them to the course which they are now pursuing." Jones went on to predict that "a great Southern army" would be "put in motion, attracting to itself the good and true men of every section" who would end Lincoln's "fanatical rule."

Everyone in the South—and in the North as well—waited anxiously to see how the unseceded slave states would officially react to Lincoln's call to arms. To the surprise and discontent of both sides, the governors of the states in question assumed Jefferson Davis' wait-and-see stance. Governor Beriah Magoffin of Kentucky sent Washington a telegram announcing, "I say emphatically, Kentucky will furnish no troops for the wicked purpose of subduing her sister Southern states." But the pompous politico then proceeded to straddle the fence—a balancing act that he would manage to keep up without falling for several months. Maryland and Missouri declined to send Lincoln troops,

Scruffy backwoodsmen of the 9th Mississippi Infantry gather round a campfire near Pensacola, Florida. Their unsoldierly mien prompted a British journalist to call them "great long-bearded fellows in flannel shirts and slouched hats, uniformless in all save brightly burnished arms and resolute purpose."

but they announced no immediate move toward secession.

The response of Virginia, which had been contemplating secession for more than two months, was watched most closely: This was the richest and most populous Southern state, and many a shrewd observer on either side assumed that North Carolina and Tennessee would quickly follow the Old Dominion's lead.

Virginia, on receiving Lincoln's call to arms, could hardly wait to get out of the Union; Virginians told one another they would never stand for such crass, arrogant threats, and that they would never assist in coercing their fellow Southerners. Just two

days later, on the 17th of April, a state convention in Richmond passed an ordinance of secession, and though the popular vote to decide the issue would not come until May 23, secession was henceforth a foregone conclusion. What is more, Governor John Letcher of Virginia immediately began acting against the federal government with an aggressiveness that surely brought a wan smile to President Davis' lips.

On April 18, a Virginia militia unit under Captain Turner Ashby moved swiftly to take the U.S. arsenal at Harpers Ferry. The small Union garrison there judged the place indefensible, for it was ringed by hills and high bluffs from which an attacker could bom-

Sentimental Farewells to the Gallant Recruits

The heart-wrenching start of the Civil War came at a time when Americans wore their hearts on their sleeves. It was the springtime of American innocence, when most people believed without question in the ideals and morals they had been taught at school, church and family hearth. And they expressed their beliefs with unabashed emotion, in flowery prose, tear-streaked poetry and cloying, sentimental art.

An endless stream of mawkish domestic scenes, painted for sheet-music covers or lithographs, attests to the fierce patriotism that animated both sides in April 1861. Several paintings show a young woman sewing a uniform for her volunteer or "consecrating" (i.e., kissing) his sword or battle flag. As one work indicated, young men who did not volunteer were scorned: In it, a woman's father refuses her hand to a suitor in civilian clothes. The volunteer's departure was another favorite theme. Inevitably, a tear-jerking picture portrayed a family at dinner and focused on an empty chair, recently vacated by some patriot who had gone a-soldiering.

Poetry in praise of the battle-bound volunteer was hardly less maudlin. The paeans invariably included, as did a Confederate woman's, the information that the beholder's "eyes fill to witness such noble resolution." A New York poet pictured "a farewell group weeping at every cottage" as Union militiamen marched off "with hearts too full for utterance, with but a single tear."

Yet the spirit of the time was genuinely heroic, and some contemporaries captured it with true grandeur. Oliver Wendell Holmes Jr., a lieutenant of Massachusetts troops in 1861 (and later Associate Justice of the United States Supreme Court), wrote of his war-torn generation: "Through our great good fortune, in our youth our hearts were touched with fire. It was given to us to learn at the outset that life is a profound and passionate thing. We have seen with our own eyes the snowy heights of honor, and it is for us to report to those who come after us."

A painting titled *The Consecration—1861* shows the demure sweetheart of a rose-sniffing officer dedicating his sword to the Union cause. This work, by Philadelphian George Lambdin, was praised in its time for its "genuine sentiment."

A stalwart Southern youth bids adieu to the old plantation in a work by Tennessee painter Gilbert Gaul. The wartime genre of sentimental domestic scenes remained popular for half a century after the War.

bard the town. So the troops set fire to some 15,000 weapons and then retreated in haste across the Potomac River to Hagerstown, Maryland. When the Virginians marched in, they found—to their delight—more than 5,000 usable rifles and the parts for many more. The armory's rifle-making machinery was captured intact.

Two days later, other Virginia troops advanced on the important Gosport Navy Yard near Norfolk. The Union commander at Norfolk, elderly Commodore Charles S. McCauley, was intimidated by disloyal subordinates; on hearing reports that Virginia troops were closing in, he hastily ordered his men to scuttle or burn all the warships in port that could not put out to sea. Only three vessels got away. The others came to rest broken and charred—but not irredeemable—on the shallow bottom of the Elizabeth River. The Rebels would salvage the burned-out hulk of the U.S.S. *Merrimack*, refit it, and send it out as the ironclad C.S.S.

Virginia to haunt the Union. More important, the Federals lost more than 1,000 heavy naval guns, which the Confederates would distribute to bolster fortifications throughout their territory. The Federals also bungled the job of destroying the Navy Yard's facilities, and, without a fight, the Virginians assumed command of one of the best naval stations in the country.

Davis and the Confederacy did suffer a palpable defeat that April, at Fort Pickens off Pensacola, Florida. There had been an armistice of sorts at Pickens since January, the Federals refraining from reinforcing the place as long as the Confederates did not attack. But the Confederate siege of Fort Sumter had voided all such agreements as far as Lincoln was concerned, and Fort Pickens was immediately resupplied and reinforced.

Davis' reaction was a measure of the ideological gulf that separated him from Lincoln and the South from the North. Davis and his government felt betrayed. They saw their

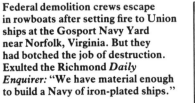

Federal demolition crews escape in rowboats after setting fire to Union ships at the Gosport Navy Yard near Norfolk, Virginia. But they had botched the job of destruction. Exulted the Richmond *Daily Enquirer:* "We have material enough to build a Navy of iron-plated ships."

capture of Fort Sumter as a legal and just repossession of South Carolina property on loan to the federal government, and thus they considered Lincoln's reinforcement of Pickens to be an unprovoked act of war. Had he guessed that Lincoln would take such underhanded action, Davis said, he would have ordered an attack on Fort Pickens as well as Sumter. For the rest of his days, he denounced Lincoln's "perfidy."

Despite the little reverse at Fort Pickens, the tide that April was running strongly in favor of the Confederacy, and a giddy sense of victory hung in the soft Southern air. Excitement mounted as regiments from all over Virginia, and more and more from all over the South, flooded into Richmond, the collection area for the presumed battlefields of northern Virginia. "From the ardor of the volunteers already beginning to pour into the city," wrote John B. Jones, a former Philadelphia editor who had defected to the Confederacy, "I believe 25,000 men could be collected and armed in a week." Two days later Jones revised his estimate upward to 50,000. "Every hour there are fresh arrivals of organized companies from the country," he wrote. "Martial music is heard everywhere, day and night, and all the trappings and paraphernalia of war's decorations are in great demand."

Davis and Confederate officials, encouraged by Virginia's zeal for the fray and anxious to demonstrate their commitment to the defense of the state, opened negotiations to move the Confederate capital from small, remote Montgomery to the larger and more accessible capital of the Old Dominion. The transfer would be completed on the 29th of May, when President Davis himself arrived in Richmond.

Meanwhile, on April 29, Jefferson Davis delivered to the Confederate Congress what was undoubtedly the most optimistic and openly emotional speech he ever made. By that time more than 62,000 Southern soldiers had been raised and were in training, and 15,000 more were on their way from the various home states to northern Virginia and other key points. "A people thus united and resolute," he proclaimed, "cannot shrink from any sacrifice which they may be called on to make, nor can there be a reasonable doubt of their final success." Davis reiterated that Southerners had taken up arms only to defend themselves against Yankee aggression and attempts to coerce them back into the Union. "The moment that this pretension is abandoned, the sword will drop from our grasp," but "so long as this pretension is maintained, with a firm reliance on that Divine Power which covers with its protection the just cause, we will continue to struggle for our inherent right to freedom, independence, and self-government."

The movement toward secession continued. On May 1 the Tennessee legislature passed a military alliance with the Confederacy, though the state would not actually secede until June 8, 1861. Arkansas left the Union on May 6, and when North Carolina followed on the 20th, the 11-state Confederacy was complete.

The city of Washington, whose population had reached 61,000 in 1860, spent the first two weeks of the War teetering on the brink of panic. Lucius E. Chittenden, a Vermont banker and prominent Lincoln supporter who arrived in the capital on April 17 to serve as Register of the Treasury, found every main thoroughfare blocked and guarded; he

wrote that Washington wore "the aspects of a besieged town" and was "filled with flying rumors of various descriptions." One wild report told of ships steaming up the Potomac loaded with Rebel cutthroats. Other tales had it that 5,000 armed men, or even 10,000, were on their way to attack the city or hijack the federal government.

Chittenden, whose sense of the Union's strength had been bolstered by the fervent patriotic displays he had seen in Northern cities on his journey south, was jolted to find that his government was weak, frightened and ill-prepared to defend the capital. No more than 1,000 troops of the nation's scattered 13,000-man Regular Army were on hand; they had the backing of 1,500 militiamen, but this number included many Southern sympathizers who were considered untrustworthy. For Chittenden, the greatest shock came on April 18, when he was assigned to help issue weapons and ammunition to the Treasury clerks in case of an enemy attack. Because the Treasury Building was considered Washington's strongest, it had been decided that Lincoln and his Cabinet would take refuge there during any Confederate assault, and Chittenden realized with horror that he might be called upon to defend his President with his own hands.

In fact, the capital stood in no immediate military peril. Any serious attack on Washington would require a substantial amount of manpower and equipment—plus time to organize, train and mount the expedition. The governments in Richmond and Montgomery simply were not ready.

Nonetheless, Washington was in real danger—albeit danger of another kind, and from the opposite direction. The 10-square-mile District of Columbia was pinned against

the Potomac and engulfed on all other sides by Maryland; if that state joined Virginia in secession, Washington might well lose its land routes and communication links to loyal states in the north and west. The Union could hardly function well without its head.

Moreover, Northerners had little reason to think that Maryland would stay in the Union. Marylanders did more than one third of their business with their fellow slave states. And there was alarming evidence of the state's disenchantment with the Union. In the presidential election of 1860, Abraham Lincoln, running on his save-the-Union pledge, received fewer than 3,000 of the 92,000-odd votes cast in the state; the city of Baltimore, where rail lines from the north and west connected with the single line to Washington, gave Lincoln just a little more than 1,000 of its 31,000 votes. To some ex-

Colonel Gaston Coppens' Louisiana Zouaves line up to receive a drink from their pretty provisioner, or *vivandière (left)*. The unit, a polyglot collection of mainly French-speaking volunteers, adopted the exotic costume of the famous French Zouave regiments that served in Algeria.

April 18 was more reassuring than alarming. Most of the men were unarmed and poorly trained. Worse, they told cautionary tales of their trip through Baltimore: A jeering mob of secessionists had pelted them with rocks and paving stones. In any event, the Pennsylvanians contributed handsomely to the bizarre makeshifts that war foisted on Washington. Since there were no barracks in the city, the troops were quartered in the Capitol and were fed meals from an emergency kitchen set up in the basement.

The next regiment scheduled to reach Washington was the 6th Massachusetts Infantry. This volunteer unit was one of four that had been drilling in the Bay State for several months on the assumption that the secession of the Southern states had made war inevitable. The regiments' commander was a brilliant, unscrupulous and exceedingly powerful Lowell attorney named Benjamin F. Butler, who had tirelessly helped organize these militia units but had never led so much as a squad into battle. It was then standard practice for a governor to reward or solicit important backers with appointments to high posts in the state militia, regardless of their military qualifications. On both sides, but especially the North, many political generals who took to the field would prove to be a curse.

Word of his appointment by Massachusetts Governor John Andrew reached Butler while he was in the midst of a trial. "I am called to prepare troops to be sent to Washington," the brand-new brigadier general announced importantly in the courtroom, and the case being argued was postponed, never to be finished. Directing operations from Boston, Butler shipped two of his regiments to strategic Fort Monroe near Hamp-

tent, the figures were deceptive: Most Marylanders probably preferred the Union to the Confederacy. But pro-Union Marylanders, among them the vacillating Governor Thomas H. Hicks, were apparently intimidated by the more militant secessionists, who were strongest around Baltimore, in central Maryland and on the Eastern Shore.

Actually, it made no difference whether Washington was endangered from the south or from the north; the best counter to both threats was to bring soldiers to the capital, as many as possible and as soon as possible. On the day Lincoln sounded the call to arms, he voiced a special appeal for troops to the nearby state of Pennsylvania and was quickly obliged with a token shipment of a few hundred men.

It was questionable, though, whether the Pennsylvanians' arrival from Harrisburg on

Cheered by thousands of well-wishers, soldiers of the elite 7th New York Militia parade down Broadway en route to Washington on the 19th of April, 1861. "It was worth a life, that march," wrote a young private, who would pay exactly that price less than two months later.

ton Roads, Virginia. Then, leaving the 8th Massachusetts at home to complete its organization and equipping, he sent the 6th Massachusetts to the capital under the command of Colonel Edward F. Jones, a 32-year-old former businessman from Utica, New York.

Jones and his regiment boarded a train for New York on April 17 and arrived the next day to a tumultuous reception. The men marched down Broadway, cheered by thousands, then were treated to a lavish meal at the Astor House. That night they continued their journey via Philadelphia, intent upon completing the trip to Washington on the morrow. Some time before Jones loaded his regiment on 10 coaches in the Philadelphia rail yards in the early hours of April 19, he received word of the hostile reception Baltimore had given the Pennsylvanians. He distributed ammunition and ordered his men to load their weapons.

The train reached Baltimore's President Street station around noon. This was the terminus of the Philadelphia, Wilmington & Baltimore line, and for travelers bound farther south, horses would pull their railroad cars over a track through the city to the Camden Street station, where the Baltimore & Ohio line to Washington commenced.

At the President Street station, Colonel Jones made a critical mistake. Instead of detraining his 800-man regiment and marching it in a compact column through the city, he instructed the troops to ride their slow-moving coaches to Camden Street. As a result of this order the soldiers were sitting targets, with no opportunity for quick deployment or maneuver. Moreover, the regiment could be split up.

The first seven cars arrived at Camden Street quickly and without mishap. But the last three cars were slowed down by a crowd that grew to perhaps 8,000 as the citizens learned what was happening. At Pratt Street, the mob halted the horses, and the Bay Staters were forced to pile out and march for their lives. Before long the men were hurrying through a hail of missiles. Soon bystanders began to wrestle with them, wrenching their muskets from their hands. Then pistol shots rang out.

Moments later, a soldier in the front rank fell, killed by a civilian's bullet. At that, the officer in charge ordered his men to return fire. Their fusillade cut a path through the mob, and the companies completed the march at a quickstep, helped rather tardily by the pro-secessionist Baltimore police.

At the Camden Street station, Colonel Jones was enraged by the rattle of gunfire, and as his beleaguered rear elements rejoined him, he tried to form the regiment for an attack on the mob. Cooler heads dissuaded him, however, and the troops crowded aboard the railroad cars bound for Washington. A locomotive was attached, and they set off for the capital, leaving behind three soldiers and 12 civilians dead, more than 20 troops injured and 130 unaccounted for. When the train finally pulled into the capital at 5 o'clock in the afternoon, Lincoln himself was there to meet it. Shaking Jones's hand, he said, "Thank God you have come."

Lincoln's problems with Baltimore and Maryland were not over—far from it. Governor Hicks, buckling under to secessionist leaders, agreed that the best way to keep the peace was to keep the troublesome Yankee troops out of the state. Gangs of secessionists quickly acted on this conclusion, demolishing four railroad bridges leading to Baltimore. The destroyed bridges, together with

Pennsylvanians to the Rescue

When Abraham Lincoln issued his call to arms on April 15, 1861, his friend and political ally, Governor Andrew G. Curtin of Pennsylvania, rushed five militia companies to the defense of Washington. These volunteer units, among them the well-drilled Ringgold Light Artillery, arrived on April 18. They were the first troops from any state to reach the capital, and Washingtonians welcomed them with relief and jubilation.

But from that moment on, misfortune dogged the 100-odd Ringgold soldiers. In the hasty trip south they had left their four cannon behind, and much to their indignation

PENNSYLVANIA GOVERNOR ANDREW G. CURTIN

the artillerymen were handed muskets just as though they were ordinary infantrymen. Worse, the authorities put them to work building fortifications and barricading the Washington riverfront with barrels of flour and cement and sheets of boiler iron. Later the men were sent to the Washington Navy Yard and Arsenal to defend against an expected Confederate invasion, which never took place. Finally, in mid-July, their 90-day enlistment expired and, without having fired a single shot at the enemy, the disgusted patriots of the Ringgold Light Artillery packed up and headed home.

This hand-painted silk flag was proudly borne by the men of the Ringgold Light Artillery during their brief tour of duty in Washington.

Training as infantry, the Ringgold artillerymen drill in a column of fours at the Washington Navy Yard on the Anacostia River.

25

the losses suffered by the 6th Massachusetts in transit, temporarily halted Lincoln's efforts to squeeze troops through the Baltimore bottleneck. Reinforcements for Washington would have to come by another route.

The most promising alternative was to send regiments by ship from northern ports to Annapolis, on the Chesapeake Bay 20 miles south of Baltimore. From there the troops could march overland 40 miles to Washington. Embarkation orders went out to the 7th New York, a fine parade regiment, and several units from Rhode Island.

Hearing of this, Maryland secessionists threatened to block the new route, and when representatives were called to the White House, they demanded that Union soldiers cease defiling the state's sacred soil. Lincoln refused. "I *must* have troops for the defense of the capital," he told the delegation, which included Mayor George W. Brown of Baltimore and the Police Marshal of Baltimore, George P. Kane. Lincoln went on, "Our men are not moles and can't dig under the earth; they are not birds and can't fly through the air. There is no way but to march them across, and that they must do." He concluded with a lame warning: "Keep your rowdies in Baltimore and there will be no bloodshed." In other words, the President of the United States had no choice but to abandon Maryland's first city to secessionist rabble in the hope of quarantining the state's rebellion.

The sea-land route was long and slow, and days passed in Washington with no sign of the promised regiments. The President was frequently seen by his secretaries anxiously pacing about his office, and he was heard muttering, "Why don't they come? Why don't they come?" During a visit to the men of the 6th Massachusetts, who were billeted with the Pennsylvanians in the Capitol, the President uncharacteristically allowed his frustration to show in public: "I don't believe there is any North!" he exclaimed. "The 7th Regiment is a myth! Rhode Island is not known in our geography any longer! You are the only Northern realities!"

Lincoln's mainstay during the uncertain days of late April was Winfield Scott, the General in Chief of the Army. Scott had been a national hero since the infancy of the republic, had commanded the American army that won the Mexican War of 1846-1848, had served in the Army for 53 years and had been its top general since 1841. The handicaps of age, poor health and enormous bulk—Scott was almost 75, matched Lincoln's height of six feet four and tipped the scales at almost 300 pounds—made it impossible for him to lead an army in the field; he had enough difficulty merely hauling his great weight up from his desk. But he stayed at that desk 16 hours a day during the crisis, calmly deploying his meager, motley forces in defense of Washington, planning strategy, sending frequent reports to the White House and doing the voluminous paperwork necessary to bring a genuine army into being. And although Scott conceded that the Confederate force of about 30,000 men at Charleston was larger than his whole army east of the frontier, he remained serenely confident that all would be well.

Because the new regiments were so slow to arrive, General Scott improvised a few colorful units of irregulars. One, made up of over-aged veterans, was aptly called the Silver Grays. Another outfit was the Clay Battalion, formed and led by a rough-and-tumble Kentucky newspaper editor and politician

Men of the 6th Massachusetts fire into a mob of rock-throwing secessionists during the Baltimore riot of April 19, 1861. One of the three soldiers killed in the melee was Private Luther Ladd (*left*), aged 17.

Navy Yard. The Clay Battalion remained on duty until May 2, when Lincoln paid tribute to Clay and sent him off to Russia.

While Lincoln and Scott waited for the troop strength in Washington to build up, they were dealt repeated cruel blows by the defection of pro-Southern officers—a trend that had kept the Army in turmoil since South Carolina began the secession movement in December 1860. Many of West Point's most brilliant graduates had felt that their first loyalty was to their home states, and had "gone South" to cast their lot with the Confederacy. Louisiana's General Pierre Gustave Toutant Beauregard, commander of the siege of Fort Sumter, had been one of the first to defect, and he was followed by the Army's highest-ranking active staff officer, Virginia-born Brigadier General Joseph E. Johnston. In all, 313 officers—nearly one third of the experienced Regulars the Army possessed—resigned to take arms against the Union. The situation was nearly as bad in the Navy. Out of 1,554 officers of all ranks, 373—or almost one fourth—left the U.S. Navy, and most of them joined the Confederate Navy.

The defection that Lincoln and Scott regretted most deeply was that of Colonel Robert E. Lee. As an officer of engineers, Lee had served brilliantly under Scott in Mexico, and Scott had followed his career with almost paternal concern ever since. Lee was the first choice of Scott and the President to lead the Union armies into battle.

On April 18, Lincoln sent an emissary to sound out Lee and judge if he would accept the command. Lee listened politely and expressed the belief that "I look upon secession as anarchy." If he owned every slave in the South, he would "sacrifice them all to the

named Cassius Marcellus Clay, whose vigorous support of Lincoln had earned him the post of Minister to Russia. Clay was in Washington waiting to depart for St. Petersburg when Sumter fell, and he went to the War Department to offer his services as an ordinary fighting man to Secretary of War Simon Cameron. "Sir," said Cameron, "this is the first instance I ever heard of where a foreign minister volunteered in the ranks." Said Clay, "Then let's make a little history."

Gathering some friends and associates, the Kentuckian formed his unit, which stood guard at the Executive Mansion and the

Struggling with a huge timber, troops of the Washington-bound 8th Massachusetts and 7th New York rebuild a sabotaged railroad bridge at Annapolis Junction, Maryland, reopening the route to the capital.

Union." But, he sadly concluded, "how can I draw my sword upon Virginia, my native state?" He would return to his home at Arlington House, just across the Potomac, "share the miseries of my people and save in defense will draw my sword on none."

After this interview, Lee went to see his friend and mentor, Scott. It was a tearful moment for them both. "Lee," said the aged general, "you have made the greatest mistake of your life, but I feared it would be so."

A number of Southern officers remained loyal to the United States—and paid a high price for their choice. Major George H. Thomas of Virginia, who was to become one of the Union's best generals, was reviled and disowned by his own family when he refused to resign his commission. General Scott, himself a Virginian, suffered cruelly for his allegiance to the Union. When the Old Dominion declared for secession on the 17th of April, many Southerners assumed that Scott

would join the Confederacy, and Governor Letcher even smuggled a delegation of Virginians into Washington to discuss with Scott his expected defection. The general cut their spokesman off in midsentence. "I have served my country, under the flag of the Union, for more than 50 years," he said, "and so long as God permits me to live, I will defend that flag with my sword, even if my own native state assails it."

Scott's decision stirred up a storm of Southern vituperation. "With the red-hot pencil of infamy," raged an editorial in the Abingdon, Virginia, *Democrat*, "he has written upon his wrinkled brow the terrible, damning word, 'Traitor.'" In Charlottesville, students at the University of Virginia burned him in effigy. His nephew tore the general's portrait from the wall of the family home and ordered his slaves to chop it up and throw it into a millpond.

Of much greater concern to General Scott

was the situation in Baltimore, which failed to improve despite the President's chary decision to bypass the city. A secessionist cut the telegraph wires from Baltimore southward, forcing Washington to rely for a while on a single line westward. Baltimore Police Marshal Kane sent out messengers in all directions to raise secessionist sharpshooters and hustle them back to town. The British consul in Baltimore reported, "The excitement and rage of everyone, of all classes and shades of opinion, was intense."

But the secessionists failed to discourage that reckless opportunist from Massachusetts, Benjamin Butler. On April 20, General Butler was in Philadelphia with his 8th Massachusetts. He heard of the violence in Baltimore and, unable to communicate with Washington, deduced that Baltimore was impassable. Clearly he had to find a way around that city. It did not take him long. He and the Massachusetts men went by train to Perryville on the banks of the Susquehanna, commandeered a big ferryboat and sailed down to Annapolis. So far so good.

Butler's plan was to travel on the Annapolis & Elk Ridge Railroad from Annapolis to Washington. However, secessionist officers of the line saw to it that a little hitch developed. To stop Butler, they sent their locomotives out of town and had work gangs tear up the rails behind them. But Butler discovered a broken-down locomotive in an abandoned shed and, on asking if anyone in his command could fix the engine, received a singularly gratifying reply. A private took a look and said, "That engine was made in our shop; I guess I can fit her up and run her." The private did so. In the meantime, Secretary of War Cameron and Thomas A. Scott, Vice President of the Pennsylva-

nia Central Railroad, assembled a group of trained railroad men—including a young Scot named Andrew Carnegie—and the railroaders repaired the tracks. The first trainload of troops chugged off toward Washington on April 25.

That day started out in doleful fashion in the capital. The news from all points was bad, and General Scott was preparing to issue an alarm saying, "From the known assemblage near this city of numerous hostile bodies of troops it is evident that an attack upon it may be expected at any moment." But instead of an attack, the city received, at about noon, the men of Butler's 8th Massachusetts and the crack 7th New York. Cheered with fraternal pride by the 6th Massachusetts and with almost hysterical relief by the citizens of Washington, the New Yorkers and the Massachusetts men paraded up Pennsylvania Avenue and past the White House grounds. President Lincoln came out to wave to them and, said an aide, "He smiled all over."

The logjam had been broken; henceforth 15,000 men a day could travel the rail line from Annapolis to Washington, and it no longer mattered so much what happened in Baltimore. But a great deal more did happen in Maryland, and once again the venturesome General Butler played a leading role in the events.

On April 26, Governor Hicks called the Maryland legislature into session at Frederick, 50 miles west of Baltimore and 18 miles northeast of Harpers Ferry. There was still a danger that secessionist agitators might panic the legislature into taking Maryland out of the Union. Frederick itself was a key point in Maryland, lying athwart the Baltimore & Ohio rail line to Harpers Ferry and the

Federal artillerymen, guarding a railroad bridge
near Relay House, watch for troublemakers from
secessionist Baltimore, eight miles to the north.
Their commander, General Benjamin F. Butler, had
no fear of an attack, declaring that he had never
seen "any force of Maryland secessionists that could
not have been overcome with a large yellow dog."

route to and from the Shenandoah Valley.

To neutralize Frederick, General Scott decided that a railway junction eight miles from Baltimore on the line to Frederick should be seized and held by Federal troops. He ordered General Butler to take the junction—called Relay House, after a local hotel—with his Massachusetts men. At about the same time, Union troops closed in on Baltimore, reinforcing Fort McHenry and garrisoning Fort Morris, and construction crews went to work restoring the sabotaged railroad bridges.

Butler's sortie to Relay House turned out to be easy. On May 5, he and the 6th Massachusetts traveled north from Washington by rail, occupied the junction and emplaced artillery batteries. In the following days, other Massachusetts units arrived at Relay House to reinforce Butler, but they were not needed. Relay House was so dull, in fact, that Butler quickly lost interest in his assigned mission. The general's natural instinct for sensation drove him toward Baltimore. Although the city had quieted down considerably since the rioting in mid-April, the secessionists there were still restless—so much so that Lincoln authorized preventive arrests and the suspension of the writ of habeas corpus along the rail line.

Butler, disdaining to seek General Scott's permission, launched a bold but complicated coup from Relay House on May 13. First, for deception, a troop train traveled west into Frederick, and along the way the men arrested the noted secessionist agitator Ross Winans. Then the train retraced its path past Relay House and steamed into Baltimore. Butler's men piled out at the Camden Street station and occupied Federal Hill, overlooking the city's ship basin. Since the Yankees arrived under cover of a violent thunderstorm, their presence was barely noticed by the Baltimoreans until the next morning, after the skies had cleared. When the citizens came outdoors, they were astonished to find nearly 1,000 Union troops and a battery of artillery glowering down at them from the harbor heights. The secessionist jig was nearly up in Baltimore.

Scott reproved Butler for acting without orders and removed him from his post. But nearly every Northerner was grateful to Butler. Though the political general had run the risk of sparking a nasty incident in Baltimore, he had faced down the secessionists with a fine show of vigor and daring—this at a time when both were in short supply in the Federal military.

Washington was now secure as the forward base for Union troops pouring in from all over the nation; thanks to the strong and prompt Federal action, there was no need to fight battles for Maryland. As a result, the armies of the Union and the Confederacy would fight out most of the great battles of the War in the 100-odd miles of rough terrain between Washington and Richmond.

A Helter-skelter Rush to Arms

It was, said a Wisconsin politician, "one of those sublime moments of patriotic exaltation when everyone seems willing to sacrifice everything for a common cause." Young men responded with almost manic enthusiasm to Lincoln's call for 75,000 volunteers on April 15, 1861. From every quarter came rousing reports: Michigan "is one vast recruiting station," and "The West is all one great Eagle-scream." As a volunteer remarked, joining the Army was like smallpox: "It's catching."

Patriotic civilians spared no effort to support the recruits and the recruitment drive. State legislatures put aside political squabbles and passed generous military appro-

A crowd of 100,000 New Yorkers jams Union Square on the 20th of April, 1861, for a war rally featuring Major Robert Anderson, the heroic commander of Fort

priations. Businessmen set up relief funds to aid the families of soldiers. But the mighty turnout of volunteers created logistics problems that took time to solve. Everything the men needed was in short supply. Food distribution was so inadequate that many men got only two meals a day, and they were lucky; in Philadelphia, soldiers had to beg food from civilians. The volunteers were billeted in crude shacks, public buildings and crowded apartments. Transportation to the battle zones was overtaxed, and many recruits found themselves moving south in slow freight cars or the reeking holds of rented steamers.

The discomfort and confusion dampened the ardor of some recruits. But the great majority of volunteers remained, as one declared, "in fine spirits, feeling like larks," and soon 16 Northern states had exceeded their quotas of volunteers. How many men were headed for Washington? A Massachusetts volunteer answered for his state, "We're *all* a-comin'!"

Sumter. Six days earlier, Anderson had brought with him from Fort Sumter the flag seen flying from the equestrian statue of George Washington (*foreground*).

Lacking uniforms and weapons, zealous Vermont volunteers at Camp Baxter in St. Johnsbury muster for a drill in their civilian clothes. Delayed by shortages and mix-ups, the first wave of Vermonters did not reach Washington for weeks, but when they arrived it was reportedly with "the strength of the hills in their marching and green sprigs in their buttonholes."

Dressed in fancy uniforms with shakos, Ohioans of the Guthrie Grays militia company snap to attention in front of Cincinnati's St. Nicholas Hotel during a march

through the city. For all their martial airs, the militia were little more than marching-and-chowder societies.

Michigan volunteers at Fort Wayne in Detroit practice forming a square, a Napoleonic infantry tactic that was used to withstand cavalry charges from any direction.

Though recruits learned the drill as part of their basic training, they rarely used it in battle; increased firepower had rendered cavalry charges against infantry obsolete.

One thousand troops of the 1st Rhode Island Infantry march past a cheering crowd to the Providence railroad station en route to Washington, D.C. On their arrival, their commanding officer, Colonel Ambrose Burnside, was told to requisition supplies for his men. Aware of how little the quartermaster had on hand, Burnside replied, "Rhode Island and her governor will attend to their wants."

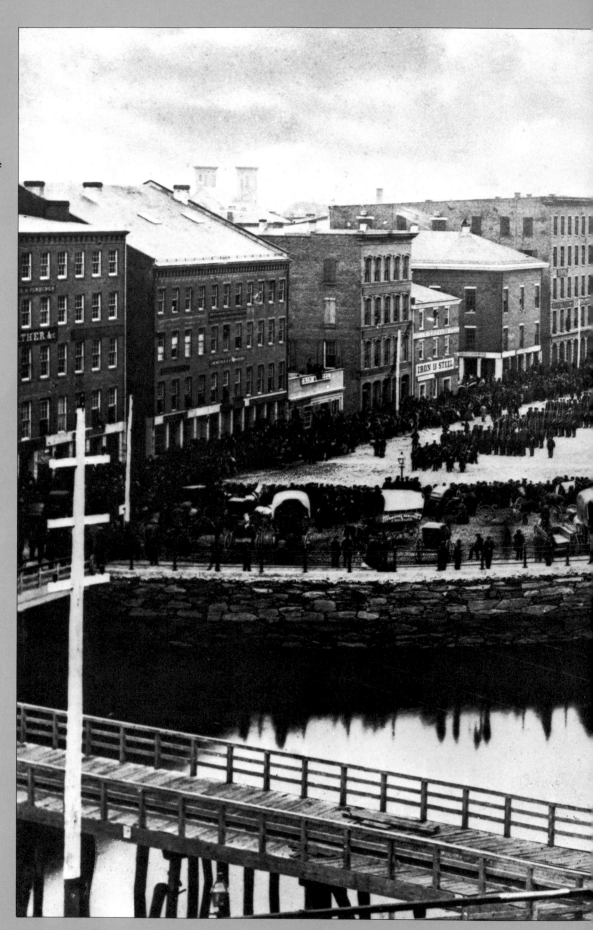

Men of the 12th New York Militia and their black servants gather in front of a ramshackle headquarters at Camp Anderson in Washington, D.C. The lieutenant seated at right, Francis Barlow, had come directly from his wedding ceremony to join his outfit on the trip south.

The Soldier's Craft

"Whether the Union stands or falls, I believe the profession of arms will henceforth be more desirable and more respected than it has been hitherto."

SENATOR CHARLES SUMNER OF MASSACHUSETTS, APRIL 1861

"I beg to lay before you," the letter read, "a plan of operations intended to relieve the pressure on Washington and tending to bring the war to a speedy close."

The writer of this self-confident sentence was the youngest general in the fast-growing Union armed forces, a 34-year-old West Pointer named George Brinton McClellan, who, after resigning his commission to go into the railroad business, had come back to serve as commander of the Ohio militia in April of 1861. The letter was sent to the General in Chief of the Army, Winfield Scott, 40 years McClellan's senior in age and in military experience. In the letter, the brash young general offered Scott two operational plans that would, he declared, swiftly and inevitably bring about "the destruction of the Southern Army."

McClellan's first plan was to gather a force of 80,000 men in the Middle West, lead them southeastward from Ohio through the mountains of western Virginia, cross the Shenandoah Valley and the Blue Ridge Mountains, and then fall upon Richmond. In his alternate plan, McClellan proposed to march his army straight south through Kentucky and Tennessee. If the army forming under Scott in Washington would cooperate, moving southward to capture the Georgia cities of Savannah and Augusta, the two Union forces could meet at a Gulf Coast port, thus splitting the Confederacy.

Scott quickly put his finger on the flaws in McClellan's strategic thinking. How was McClellan to march a huge army of unseasoned troops across hundreds of miles of hostile country, all in their three-month enlistment period? How was he to supply that army with ammunition and rations, which would have to be hauled by long trains of unwieldy horse-drawn wagons? "The general," Scott noted succinctly on the back of McClellan's letter, "eschews water transportation by the Ohio or Mississippi in favor of long, tedious, and break-down (of men, horses, and wagons) marches."

Although Scott found McClellan's suggestions ill-conceived, he welcomed the opportunity to discuss military strategy with a fellow professional; he was weary of being bombarded with amateur advice from civilians who thought the South could be defeated by a single thrust into Virginia. So Scott replied with two remarkable letters, in which he outlined his own comprehensive plan for winning the War. He foresaw that the struggle would be long and bitter, and his strategy was designed accordingly.

In his letters, Scott sought to explain not only how the Ohio and Mississippi Rivers could be used as easy avenues of supply but also how they could become the keys to ending the rebellion. He began by declaring that as President Lincoln's blockade of Southern ports took effect, it would strangle Confederate overseas trade, shutting off the vital flow of imported arms and exported cotton. "In connection with such a blockade," Scott continued, "we propose a powerful move-

THE HERCULES OF THE UNION.
SLAYING THE GREAT DRAGON OF SECESSION.

Winfield Scott, General in Chief of the Union Army, is portrayed as Hercules slaying the Hydra of secession in this 1861 cartoon. Each of the Hydra's heads bears the face of a prominent Confederate, whose alleged crime against the Union is written on his neck.

ment down the Mississippi to the ocean." An army of, say, 80,000 men would be carefully trained with four or five months of hard drill in camps along the Ohio. Part of that force would then be carried in a fleet of river steamers down the Ohio to the Mississippi; the rest would move by land while being supplied by boat. The expedition would be shepherded by a flotilla of perhaps 20 armored gunboats.

This army, with all its necessary supplies following easily by water, would proceed down the Mississippi, cleaning the Rebels from their strongholds along the banks of the great river. Combined with the sea blockade, the conquest of the Mississippi would surround the bulk of the Confederacy with Union-controlled seas or waterways. The South, in short, could be isolated and strangled into submission. And, Scott added, his scheme would achieve victory "with less bloodshed than any other plan." In any event, this bold conception of the War was to remain the only comprehensive strategy formulated by any leader on either side, North or South.

Scott naturally communicated his ideas to Lincoln and the Cabinet. Word soon leaked out, and the Northern press proceeded to denounce the scheme and its author. Fire-breathing editors such as Horace Greeley of the New York *Tribune* expected an immediate and victorious invasion of Virginia, and they derisively called Scott's slow, undramatic strategy the "Anaconda Plan," after the big constrictor snake of that name. Several editorials implied that Scott must be either senile or pusillanimous if he would settle for such a tedious, ungallant approach. Scott himself noted that "the greatest obstacle in the way of the plan" was "the impatience of

our patriotic and loyal Union friends. They will urge instant and vigorous action, regardless, I fear, of consequences."

Scott's Anaconda nevertheless proved in the long run to have a crucial, constructive influence on the Union's conduct of the War. It convinced Lincoln of the military importance of the Mississippi, and although the President and the generals who succeeded the ailing Scott never followed the Anaconda strategy consistently, the significance it attached to the capture of Rebel strongholds along the river—New Orleans, Vicksburg and others—became a fundamental part of the North's evolving war plans.

No one knew whether, or to what extent, Scott's strategic planning took into account the North's very considerable material advantages in the War. President Jefferson Davis' lack of a comprehensive strategy and his persistence in relying on defensive reactions to Northern attacks suggest that he gave little thought to the Confederacy's disadvantages. In fact, a long war of the sort that Scott foresaw would distinctly favor the Union.

In almost every aspect, the North possessed preponderant strength that could only increase as the War lengthened. Two thirds of America's 32 million people lived in the Northern states; the South had barely 9 million people, and more than a third of them were slaves, disqualified from military service by the whites' fears of armed insurrection. Of the able-bodied men between the ages of 18 and 45, the Union could draw upon 3.5 million, more than three times the total of eligible Southerners. However, slave manpower did free for combat many Southern whites who would otherwise have served only as support personnel.

The North's industrial might made the

Confederacy look pitiful. New York State alone had more factories than all the South. In addition, the free states outstripped the slave states in food crops and livestock production; the South enjoyed superiority only in rice and cotton.

For distributing what it did produce, the Confederacy possessed merely one third of the Union's rail transportation. A single direct rail route connected Richmond with the Mississippi, and the South's meager rail network was cursed with varying track gauges, which made transferring cars and engines from one line to another impossible. By contrast, nearly all of the North's railroad mileage was of uniform gauge.

However, the fact that the Confederates would be operating defensively in their home states gave them one clear advantage: Their lines of communication would be shorter than those of the Northern invaders. In addition to the efficiencies that this permitted, the Confederates would need fewer troops to guard the lines of communication and could use a larger percentage of their military manpower as fighting men. Then, too, the poor roads in the South would not hamper the Confederate armies as much as they would the more heavily laden Federal forces.

Still, Confederate confidence was based very largely on intangibles. The Southern armies would be defending their homeland, and that would give them an advantage in morale and in operating among a partisan civilian population. Furthermore, Davis expected England and France to intercede in the South's behalf, so as to guarantee themselves a steady supply of cotton from the world's greatest grower of the fiber. Pure self-interest, he thought, would impel both nations to accord the Confederacy diplomat-ic recognition, together with economic and military aid. In addition, France would sympathize with the ideals of the fledgling republic, just as the French had aided the Patriots during the Revolution. History would repeat itself, Davis believed.

The Confederates were not particularly worried about their deficiencies in war production. Besides the weapons and munitions they would import, they had already seized large supplies from Federal arsenals. Confederate agents were purchasing guns and ammunition from cynical Yankee manufacturers, who were only too happy to sell weapons to anyone at good cash prices. In time, the great Tredegar Iron Works in Richmond would become a major supplier of cannon and armor plate.

Lastly, the Confederates felt that Southerners made better soldiers than Northerners. Surely drab city shopkeepers and toilsome Yankee farmers would be no match for the plantation-bred cavaliers of the South, men who had been taught to ride and shoot as a part of their upbringing. Although this comforting notion proved untrue, Southern men did start the War with a distinct military edge: A larger percentage of them had attended military school, and therefore a larger percentage of Southern officers had some formal military education.

It was possible that President Davis' passive war policy might triumph; if a stout Southern defense repelled invasion and inflicted heavy losses, and if the Confederate armies remained intact and dangerous, the Northerners might lose heart and abandon the War. Yet thoughtful Southerners who paused to contemplate the North's huge advantages in manpower and industrial capacity concluded that a long war would play into

America's grand old military hero, General Winfield Scott began his brilliant career as a dashing young officer (*above*) in the War of 1812 and went on to command the army that captured Mexico City in 1847. But by 1861, Scott was plagued by infirmities that would soon force him to retire.

Yankee hands. The Federal armies could only become larger and stronger, the Confederate armies only smaller and weaker. To them, it seemed that the Confederacy's only hope would be to win the War before the Union could fully mobilize its strength. Said one Southern skeptic: "What we have to do must be done quickly. The longer we have them to fight, the more difficult they will be to defeat."

Nevertheless, there was a powerful historical argument against Scott's strategy. The career of the greatest modern military commander, Napoleon Bonaparte, seemed to prove that wars were won not by slowly sapping an enemy's power to wage war, but by destroying his armies in the field. Napoleon and his *Grande Armée* had repeatedly thrashed hostile European coalitions, in spite of blockades by the British Navy. Nearly every amateur strategist in the North admired Napoleon and urged the Union generals to emulate him, advancing to smash the forces of the upstart Confederates and to end the War forthwith.

Professional officers had no need for such counsel; Napoleon's career and teachings dominated military thinking in both armies and would continue to do so throughout the War. Every officer who graduated from West Point after the early 1830s had studied Napoleon's campaigns in a course on strategy and tactics taught by Professor Dennis Hart Mahan. In addition, many officers had been members of an after-hours study group called the Napoleon Club. As wartime field officers they would often pattern their battles and campaigns after Napoleon's great victories of half a century before.

According to Napoleon, the prime purpose of maneuver was to make an enemy commander believe he was menaced from two or more directions and cause him to split his force; thereupon the enemy's divided formations could be crushed successively by the entire weight of one's own army. This concentrated attack should strike the enemy's unprotected flank or the weakest point in his defensive line. It was crucial to capitalize on surprise—to attack before the enemy expected it, and with a larger force than he thought was available.

The Napoleonic keys to victory on the battlefield were speed and concentration of force—or, as the great Confederate cavalryman Nathan Bedford Forrest reputedly put it, "Git there fustest with the mostest." But any Civil War general who followed Napoleon's methods slavishly was risking disaster, for weaponry had changed radically between 1815 and 1861.

In Napoleon's time, infantry attacked on a narrow front in tight-packed columns with bayonets fixed. The columns smashed into the enemy line like battering rams, the soldiers running the defenders through, trampling them down, clambering over the bodies of dead comrades.

Such sledge-hammer attacks had succeeded largely because the standard infantry weapon used by all armies was the short-range, single-shot, slow-to-load smoothbore musket. All models of musket had to be loaded in the same laborious way: A paper cartridge containing a powder charge and a lead ball was torn open; powder and ball were dropped into the gun's muzzle, followed by the paper, which served as wadding, and the whole load was driven the length of the barrel with a ramrod. To fire the weapon, a soldier ignited the powder charge by an unreliable flintlock mechanism: A chip of flint on

A company of Union soldiers practices a drill to the rhythmic beat of a drummer (*left*). The formation, designed to repulse a cavalry charge, enabled two ranks of men to fire simultaneously and then present a solid front of bayonets.

the weapon's hammer created a spark in a shallow pan primed with a little powder from the paper cartridge. The weapon would not fire when the powder was wet or even damp. When the musket did fire (which was about 80 per cent of the time), the ball was unstable in flight and accurate only at short ranges: 200 yards against formations, up to 100 yards against individuals.

Because the musket was a short-range weapon, the Napoleonic infantrymen and cavalrymen could safely advance close to the enemy line; upon launching their charge, they would only briefly suffer losses to de-

fensive musket volleys before they began their grisly work with bayonet and saber. What was more important, the attackers' artillery could, without sustaining prohibitive losses, move far forward and pave the way for the infantry charge by blowing gaps in the enemy line.

In 1861, smoothbore muskets were still widely used. These latter-day muskets were more reliable than their antecedents, primarily because the temperamental old flintlock mechanism had been replaced by new percussion caps—cuplike copper casings containing a small amount of an explosive such as fulminate of mercury. Muskets with the percussion-cap feature were virtually certain to fire, even in foul weather.

But a far more critical improvement had transformed the musket into a rifle (*pages 70-71*). The interior of the barrel was now scored with spiral grooves. This rifling gave the bullet—a pointed lead missile instead of a lead musket ball—a stabilizing spin when it was fired. The result was a dramatic increase in the accuracy and range of the basic infantry weapon. In the hands of a good marksman, a rifle could hit an enemy soldier 600 yards away.

Armies had been reluctant to adopt the rifle for general issue, in part because the loading process was time-consuming and difficult: The powder charge had to be measured from a flask, and a tight-fitting bullet had to be rammed down the grooves. In 1849 a French Army captain named Claude E. Minié had helped introduce the first of several cone-shaped slugs with a hollow base. The new bullet was slightly smaller than the barrel's inner diameter and thus was easy to ram down; but when the bullet was fired, its base expanded to fit the rifling with requisite snugness. In deference to Minié's original design, which had since been much improved, Civil War soldiers erroneously referred to all rifle bullets as Minié balls. They continued to call their rifles muskets, and they were supplied with more and more of them as the War lengthened.

Not surprisingly, the advent of the rifle tipped the tactical balance in favor of the defense. Now infantrymen making a bayonet charge were vulnerable to rifle fire for some 500 yards before they reached the enemy's defense line, which was usually positioned at the edge of a wood or near the crest of a rise

with a long, clear field of fire ahead of it. The attacking infantrymen could not fire accurately on the run, and reloading the single-shot early rifles was a slow and difficult process (*pages 52-53*) that forced the men to stop in the open under fire. Naturally no one wanted to stop: Rifle bullets traveled at higher velocities than musket balls, and heavy slugs that did not kill outright often inflicted mortal damage to flesh and bone.

In 1861 tacticians still believed in the bayonet charge, but they gradually modified infantry tactics to take into account the power of the rifle. When preparing for a charge, the infantry approached the enemy broadside, in a line of regiments instead of in column; this extended order brought more offensive firepower to bear. Greater emphasis was placed on the deployment of skirmishers, who, instead of charging shoulder to shoulder as a mass target, spread out and became harder-to-hit individual targets. They worked their way forward from one bit of cover to the next, reloading and maintaining a sporadic fire to keep the enemy riflemen down.

The advent of the rifle caused wholesale changes in the role of the cavalry. Napoleon's horsemen, facing short-range muskets, would charge boot to boot in the wake of an infantry breakthrough or would carve out their own breakthrough in a surprise flank attack. But now the most daredevil cavalrymen seldom rode into the maelstrom of an infantry battle; the toll on the horses—not to mention the riders—was simply too great. Though the cavalry could dismount to fight when involved in a large action, it henceforth engaged chiefly in reconnaissance, in screening the movements of an army from the enemy, and in staging swift

The basic training manual for both armies was *Rifle and Light Infantry Tactics*, a pocket-sized two-volume textbook written by William J. Hardee (*above*), a former West Point commandant who joined the Confederates as a brigadier general. The maneuvers in Hardee's, such as the diagramed movement below of a regiment marching from line of battle into a column by the right flank, baffled many volunteers; by the time the Battle of Bull Run was fought, neither side had mastered them.

raids on the enemy's supply depots and lines of communication.

The longer range and greater accuracy of infantry weapons made the artilleryman's job even more hazardous than it had been before. As gun crews brought their fieldpieces forward, rifle fire slaughtered the horses that pulled the cannon. And though gunners still took delight in placing their batteries in the front line, they paid for their courage with long casualty lists.

At the outset of the War, artillery differed little from that of Napoleon's time. The French Emperor had revolutionized the use of artillery by employing light, mobile fieldpieces that could dash to any threatened spot on a battlefield. The United States Army was quick to copy and improve on the French usage with its own mobile artillery—lightweight bronze cannon mounted on rugged carriages with big wheels. By the 1840s the U.S. Army had the world's hardest-riding and swiftest-firing field artillery forces, and during the Civil War, gunners on both sides were proficient in the techniques of rapid deployment.

The fieldpieces most widely used early in the War were, like Bonaparte's guns, muzzle-loading smoothbore cannon. In offensive operations the guns' usefulness was limited. They were inaccurate at long range, whether firing solid shot—iron balls weighing six to 12 pounds—or explosive shells. At closer ranges, in support of infantry, the cannon were far more effective. They were especially deadly at ranges of around 800 yards. Case shot—hollow balls packed with powder and clusters of small iron or lead balls—cut a great swath when they exploded amid an enemy formation. Missiles called canister, which resembled tin cans filled with oversized bullets, were even more lethal, hitting lines of soldiers with the effect of giant shotgun blasts. Canister was generally used at ranges of around 300 yards, and case shot at greater ranges.

Besides their light, fast-firing smoothbore field guns, both North and South employed rifled iron cannon that could throw projectiles long distances with much-improved accuracy. The Model 1861 Ordnance rifle, which had a three-inch bore, could fire shot or shell nearly 4,000 yards, though its optimum range was around 2,400 yards. The Parrott rifle, named for inventor Robert P. Parrott, came in various sizes ranging from a 10-pounder—that is, firing a projectile weighing 10 pounds—to a mammoth 30-pounder siege gun.

Never during the Civil War would the offense catch up with the defense. But the bayonet attacks continued to the very end, even in the face of elaborate complexes of trenches and breastworks. The cost would

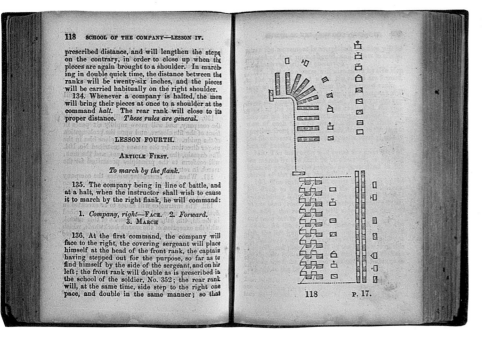

How to Load a Rifle

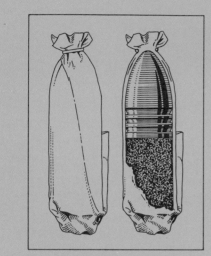

A paper cartridge, shown in cutaway at actual size, held a conical lead bullet packed atop black gunpowder. On firing, the bullet's hollow base expanded to fit the grooved bore. A sooty residue remained, making reloading harder with each shot.

In Civil War battles, attacking infantrymen typically advanced across several hundred yards of open terrain toward enemy infantrymen defending a sheltered position. The men on both sides had accurate, long-range, single-shot rifles. But the attackers were at a distinct disadvantage, since they had to stop moving to aim, fire and reload—all the while presenting an easy target. It might take minutes to reach the enemy and fire point-blank or use bayonets. These were the most terrifying minutes in a soldier's life, and for many a soldier they were the last minutes.

The worst of it was loading the rifle. This complicated, time-consuming process involved opening a paper cartridge (*left*), inserting and ramming home the bullet (called a Minié ball), and attaching a tiny percussion cap (*opposite*). The movements, which had to be made in specific order, required nimble fingers and steady nerves under the best of circumstances. Many experienced soldiers could load and fire no more than three rounds in a minute, and the heat and din of battle turned even seasoned troops into frightened fumblers. Often the rifle failed to fire, and the soldier did not know it. Of 27,000-odd rifles recovered from the Gettysburg battlefield, two thirds were loaded with two or more charges, and one contained 23. (A double charge would usually fire without mishap, but any additional charges could cause the barrel to explode or might send a blast of flame back through the firing mechanism, blinding the rifleman.)

Only one thing could prevent such mistakes and increase a soldier's efficiency in both the attack and the static defense: drill. Soldiers had to repeat, time and again, the series of steps that loaded their rifles, until they could run through the movements automatically. In teaching the drill to raw recruits, officers on both sides relied chiefly on the training manual, Hardee's *Tactics*. The steps are described below and illustrated with figures after Hardee's.

1   2   3   4   5

1 LOAD: Grasp the rifle with the left hand. Place the butt between the feet, the barrel toward the front. Seize the barrel with the left hand close to the muzzle, which should be held three inches from the body. Carry the right hand to the cartridge box on the belt.

2 HANDLE CARTRIDGE/TEAR CARTRIDGE: Seize a cartridge between the thumb and the next two fingers. Place it between the teeth. Tear the paper. Hold the cartridge upright between the thumb and first two fingers in front of and near the muzzle.

3 CHARGE CARTRIDGE: Empty the powder into the barrel. Disengage the ball from the paper with the right hand and with the thumb and first two fingers of the left. Insert the ball, with its pointed end up, into the muzzle and press it down with the right thumb.

4 DRAW RAMMER: Draw the rammer out by extending the arm. Turn the rammer. Keeping the back of the hand toward the front, place the head of the rammer on the ball.

5 RAM CARTRIDGE: Insert the rammer. Steady it with the thumb of

The weapon's firing mechanism (*left*) was armed with a copper percussion cap (*above*, *actual size*) containing half a grain of fulminate of mercury, placed on a nipple under the hammer. Pulling the trigger made the hammer crush the cap, sending a flame through the nipple into the barrel, where it set off the powder charge.

6   **7**   **8**   **9**

the left hand. Seize its small end with the thumb and forefinger of the right hand. Press the ball home, holding the elbows near the body.

6 RETURN RAMMER: Draw the rammer halfway out. Grasp it near the muzzle with the right hand. Clear

it from the bore by extending the arm. Turn it and insert it in the carrying groove. Force the rammer home by placing the little finger of the right hand on the head.

7 PRIME: With the left hand, raise the piece until the hand is as high as

the eye. Half-face to the right, with the right foot at right angles to the left. Half-cock the hammer with the thumb of the right hand. Remove the old percussion cap. Take the new cap from the pouch. Place it on the nipple. Press the cap down with the thumb.

8 READY/AIM: Fully cock the hammer and seize the small of the stock with the right hand. Place the butt against the right shoulder. Incline the head to align the right eye with the sight. Close the left eye.

9 FIRE: Press trigger with forefinger.

be terrible. In this bloodiest of American wars, the toll of soldiers who perished, of all causes, came to some 620,000—one man out of every four who served.

In basic organization, both armies were virtually identical and were not much different from those fielded by Napoleon. The regiment, commanded by a colonel, was the smallest self-contained unit of infantry. On paper, the standard Union volunteer infantry regiment had exactly 1,046 officers and men. That total included 10 companies of 101 men, each company commanded by a captain, plus the colonel's staff—an adjutant to do the paper work, a quartermaster to look after supplies and equipment, and a commissary officer to handle the feeding of the men. The regiment also had surgeons

and hospital stewards to tend the men's bodies, a chaplain to minister to their souls and a band to help them march proudly and in step. Regiments of the Confederate Army were of approximately the same size. However, few regiments on either side ever went into action at full strength. Disease, desertions, casualties and delays in replacing losses usually reduced the effective strength of most regiments by 20 per cent—and, in many cases, by a great deal more.

The average soldier gave his loyalty first to his regiment; a man took pride in belonging to the 33rd Virginia, say, or the 5th New York. Both the Union and Confederate high commands wisely realized the importance to morale of allowing state-raised regiments to maintain their state affiliations. "I would rather have no regiments raised in Ohio,"

Men of the 1st Ohio Light Artillery stand beside one of their six-pounder fieldpieces. Although cannoneers were trained to work in gun crews of eight or nine men, their drill instructions provided for fighting with diminished crews, ending ominously with "service by two men."

declared an Ohioan in Lincoln's Cabinet, "than that they should not be known as Ohio regiments." This view was heartily endorsed by the governors, who jealously guarded their prerogatives to appoint officers as political patronage.

Most Civil War engagements were so large that regiments seldom fought as independent units. Rather they marched and were deployed as brigades, usually of two to six regiments each. Three or so brigades were grouped together to make still-larger units, the divisions, and several divisions would then be combined to form an infantry corps. In the great battles to come at places like Antietam and Fredericksburg and Gettysburg, a commander would commit several entire corps to the fray—perhaps 20,000 men in 35 regiments—and send them forward as one huge unit to attack an enemy formation of similar magnitude.

For the cavalry, the regiment was again the basic unit. Union cavalry regiments, for a large part of the War, had 12 companies, sometimes called troops, each with a paper strength of 103 officers and men. A cavalry regiment, including its staff and field officers, was therefore larger than its infantry counterpart, nominally numbering 1,254. The greater size was the result of simple need. The strength of a mounted unit in battle was affected not only by the factors that cut into infantry strength but also by the condition of its animals. Ailing or exhausted horses could sap a regiment's strength in a mounted engagement. And when cavalrymen fought dismounted, as they often did, only three men out of four could actually fight; the fourth man remained in the rear to hold the horses.

The basic unit of artillery was the battery—normally six cannon and 144 men commanded by a captain or, more often, a lieutenant. Early in the War, several artillery batteries were simply attached to each infantry brigade or division. Later, anywhere from four to 12 batteries were formed into artillery brigades or battalions that were assigned to infantry corps. Eventually an artillery reserve was established—a large number of guns, under the control of the army's chief of artillery, that could be thrown into a fight at any threatened point.

In addition to the three combat arms, an army needed a host of ancillary organizations. Among these were engineers, who cut roads through the wilderness, dug earthworks and built pontoon bridges; whole regiments of specially skilled marksmen known as sharpshooters; and signalmen to estab-

Playful volunteers of the 7th New York Militia build a human pyramid in an off-duty period. But the soldiers' tough training schedules left little time for clowning; they drilled by company and regiment as often as five times a day, seven days a week.

lish observation posts and oversee communications. Many specialists were required to operate the tools of war made available by recent technological advances: telegraphers and wire-laying gangs for the telegraph equipment that provided virtually instantaneous communication between widely separated armies; crewmen of the U.S. Military Railroad to handle the trains that could speedily transfer troops and supplies from one scene of battle to another. In short, the armies of the North and the South began the War as products of a Napoleonic heritage, but they evolved, during four years of battle, into the first modern armies.

Although the Federal and Confederate Armies were practically identical in the matters of structure, weaponry and tactical principles, they differed significantly in one respect. Despite the fact that the Confederate Army was being built from scratch, its officer corps was better than that of the well-established Union Army. This disparity grew more and more obvious in the spring and early summer of 1861, as both sides struggled to organize, train and bring to battle their proliferating forces.

There were a number of reasons for the superiority of the Confederate officer staff. The West Pointers who "went South" included an especially large and talented group of high-level officers. A disproportionately large number of the other Confederate officers had had at least a modicum of formal military education. But, paradoxically, the most important reason of all was that the Confederate officer corps lacked what seemed to be the main strength of the Federal officer corps: a large cadre of experienced seniors. Henry W. Halleck, who would serve

as the chief general of the Union armies during the Civil War, recognized the problem when he was a lieutenant in 1846. He wrote: "In the event of another war, shall we again exhume the veterans of former days, and again place at the head of our armies respectable and aged inefficiency? Or shall we seek out youthful enterprise and activity combined with military science and instruction? The results of the war, the honor of the country, the glory of our arms, depend, in great measure, upon the answer that will be given to this question."

It was a question that every nation faced during long periods of peace, when the army shriveled in size and its officers, whatever their proven merits as leaders and fighting men, grew old and conservative, clogging the pathway to promotion for the younger, more vigorous officers. The seniority system, which awarded promotions more by length of service than for present ability, made the Union Army especially attractive to elderly timeservers. Conversely, the Confederate Army was particularly alluring to daring and energetic young officers who aspired to make the most of their generation's war. As the early battles of the War would show, the daring, energy and just plain belligerence of the Confederate officer corps had much to do with Confederate successes.

The Union Army, far from encouraging its young officers to show their mettle, inadvertently discouraged them in various ways. Political appointments raised a number of unqualified civilians to high rank in state militias, thwarting the careers of promising young officers. Of course the Southern states had their own political generals and colonels, but fewer than the Northern states.

In the North, moreover, young Regular

Army officers were required to resign their commissions before they could accept appointments to higher ranks in the state-organized volunteer units. Since this meant losing their seniority, many highly qualified junior officers declined promotion and resigned themselves to serving in minor capacities. A year passed before regulations were changed to permit capable young West Point lieutenants to accept promotions to brigadier general, colonel or major in volunteer outfits without losing their Regular Army rank.

The discrepancies in quality between the Federal and Confederate officer staffs were most pronounced at the regimental level. The colonels commanding volunteer regiments, which made up the bulk of both armies, bore the responsibility of molding raw recruits into competent soldiers. It was their task to oversee training in weaponry, marching and battlefield maneuver. The training was not so much complicated as it was time-consuming; the soldiers had to repeat their drills time and again until they obeyed orders instantly and without thought. Too often, regimental commanders neglected the job.

To make up for weary or lethargic or incompetent colonels, vigorous young West Point graduates were temporarily assigned to the hard work of drilling and training the recruits. But no matter how well a lieutenant performed this task, he often received as his only immediate reward the tragic decimation of the unit by his colonel's egregious battlefield blunders.

On the other hand, the commanders of the Confederate Army were untrammeled by a long list of senior officers waiting patiently for promotion, and they did not have to cope with the Union Army's ponderous bureaucracy, accumulated regulations and circumscribing traditions. President Davis, himself trained at West Point and a former United States Secretary of War, and his chief military adviser, General Robert E. Lee, looked not so much for unexceptional veterans as for exceptional fighters. They were free to gamble on their own judgment of men, and their intuitions were keen. They found a large number of talented brigade and regimental commanders in their 30s—several years younger, on the average, than their Union counterparts.

For their field commanders in the East, Davis and Lee in May 1861 chose two officers of excellent credentials. Brigadier General Pierre Gustave Toutant Beauregard, a 43-year-old Louisiana Frenchman who had become a hero of the South for his capture of Fort Sumter, was appointed commander of a Confederate army that was building around Manassas Junction, a sleepy town where rail lines running from Alexandria and from the Shenandoah Valley crossed with rails leading south from Washington to Richmond. From this key position, Beauregard was to protect northern Virginia from any incursion by Federal forces.

Also in May, Davis and Lee appointed Joseph E. Johnston, a distinguished 54-year-old veteran who held the rank of brigadier general in the Confederate Army, to command an army then being raised in the Shenandoah Valley, guarding Virginia's rugged western flank. Johnston's army was separated from Beauregard's by 50 miles and the Blue Ridge Mountains, but the Manassas Gap Railroad could quickly deliver reinforcements from either force if the other was threatened.

By late May, President Lincoln and General Scott had appointed commanders to key

Eastern posts. First they turned to Robert Patterson, a 68-year-old major general of militia who had led sizable bodies of troops under Scott during the Mexican War; it was thought that his experience might make up for his lack of youthful energy. Scott first assigned him to what was essentially a desk job, placing him in charge of a large military department that included Pennsylvania, Maryland, Delaware and the District of Columbia. When that responsibility appeared to overtax Patterson, Scott assigned the Washington sector of the territory to another old colleague, Colonel Joseph K. F. Mansfield, 58 years old.

These moves did nothing to solve the problem of who should command in the field. Age and infirmity disqualified Scott and the three other senior Regular Army officers who had remained loyal to the Union. In the absence of an outstanding candidate, Lincoln and Scott allowed the choice to be decided by politics. The vigorous Governor of Ohio, William Dennison, was busily promoting the careers of two professional soldiers from his state. One was George B. McClellan, the ambitious young strategist who had proposed a scheme for invading Virginia from the west. Dennison lobbied for him so successfully that McClellan was quickly promoted from a major general of state volunteers to a major general in the Regular Army, charged with overseeing all operations in the Middle West.

Governor Dennison's second Ohio candidate for appointment to a high Army post was Irvin McDowell, a 42-year-old brevet (acting) major who had served creditably in the Mexican War and who now held down a desk job in the Adjutant General's office. Thanks to Dennison and to strenuous wire-

This young private, name unknown, was a member of the Old Dominion Rifles, one of five Virginia militia companies to retreat from Alexandria when Union troops invaded the state on May 24, 1861. This "cased" (backed and framed) photograph is an ambrotype—a see-through glass negative whose dark background makes it resemble a positive print.

pulling by Secretary of the Treasury Salmon P. Chase, who had practiced law in Ohio, McDowell was made a Regular Army brigadier general and assigned the top field command in the East. He would lead the army of some 30,000 men that was now forming around Washington, and he would carry on his shoulders the onerous duty of invading Virginia to quash the rebellion.

Just before McDowell assumed his new command, the troops who had gathered to protect Washington made their first offensive move. On May 23, Virginians voted in a popular referendum and ratified a previous convention vote in favor of secession, making their state a member of the Confederacy. With the Old Dominion now officially enemy territory, Generals Scott and Mansfield acted with surprising swiftness. The next day, they threw 11 regiments across the Potomac to seize and hold a buffer zone for the capital.

The operation was carried out with a

At a camp near Alexandria, Virginia, the baggy-trousered 11th New York Fire Zouaves are welcomed by Colonel Marshall Lefferts of the 7th New York Militia on May 25, 1861.

smooth efficiency, but it was nevertheless an exciting event for the green troops who took part. At exactly 2 o'clock on the morning of May 24, under a brilliant moon, three columns of infantry, supported by some artillery, folded back the thin line of Confederate pickets on the Virginia side of the river. On the right flank were three New York regiments, which crossed the river upstream from Washington by the roadway atop the Potomac Aqueduct, a span connecting Georgetown, on the Washington side, and the northern end of Arlington, in Virginia. These troops then pushed two miles into Virginia, cutting the Loudoun & Hampshire rail line that connected Alexandria with the town of Leesburg, 30 miles to the west.

Two other Union columns crossed by way of the Long Bridge from Washington to Arlington. One column, commanded by a major general of New York militia, Charles Sandford, captured Arlington Heights, a vantage point from which Virginia militia had been observing activities in the capital. The Confederates swiftly retreated and Sandford's advance guard reached the Columbia Turnpike, one of the area's main thoroughfares. The Union soldiers occu-

Officers of the Irish 69th New York Militia surround an 8-inch seacoast howitzer at Fort Corcoran in Arlington, Virginia. The unit commander and namesake of the fort, Colonel Michael Corcoran (*far left*), was later captured by the Confederates at Bull Run and held prisoner for more than a year.

pied, among other useful structures, the home of Robert E. Lee, a spacious, columned mansion atop one of the highest hills in Arlington. Lee and his wife, already in Richmond, had left the place in the care of servants. "I would, by occupying it myself," said General Sandford in an official report penned in the comfort of Lee's parlor, "be responsible for the perfect care and security of the house and everything in and about it." He was but the first of a string of Union officers who would find it convenient to oversee the defense of Washington from the enemy commander's commodious home.

The other column to cross the Potomac on the Long Bridge was made up primarily of Colonel Orlando B. Willcox's 1st Michigan Regiment. On the Virginia side, these soldiers turned southeastward and set off in pursuit of a group of Rebel horsemen who, flushed from their Arlington bivouac, were speeding toward the small but important port town of Alexandria to raise the alarm. Alexandria was occupied by some 700 locally recruited Virginia militia.

Willcox had been ordered to capture the town and, if possible, its Rebel garrison. To help him, the 11th New York—an exotically clad Zouave regiment led by an immensely popular young colonel named Elmer E. Ellsworth—was to be landed in Alexandria by three river steamers, with the sloop of war *Pawnee* as their escort.

The alarm was given, as it turned out, not by the fast-riding Confederate troopers, but by a Union Naval officer from the *Pawnee;* he went ashore well before Ellsworth's scheduled dawn landing and—apparently with no authorization—offered the commander of the Alexandria garrison, Colonel

George H. Terrett, a truce until 9 o'clock if he would withdraw his troops peaceably. His motive, the Navy man said, was to spare the women and children of the town any risk from gunfire.

Given this more-than-fair warning, Terrett was able to assemble his troops near Alexandria's main intersection of Washington and King Streets, several blocks from the waterfront. This was no easy feat, since the Rebel soldiers were billeted all over town in their own homes. Terrett's ill-armed force—it had no more than two bullets per man—moved toward the nearby depot of the Orange & Alexandria Railroad just as Willcox's Michigan infantry marched into the town from the north and the 11th New York came ashore from their ships. Willcox later recalled that his men "exchanged a few shots with their vanishing rear guard," but the main body of Terrett's troops got safely aboard some railway cars and escaped. The Federals were able to capture only 35 dawdling Rebel horsemen.

During the operation, the Union side suffered a stunning loss: Colonel Ellsworth, the Zouave commander, was killed (*pages 62-69*). Nevertheless, the Yankee success was, as a reporter for the Washington *Evening Star* wrote, "a stirring one indeed." The next morning the exhilarated Federal troops on the Potomac's southern bank set to work erecting what would become an intricate system of fortifications protecting the capital.

As more troops crossed the bridges to encamp on Virginia soil, their newly minted brigadier general, Irvin McDowell, rode to join them. There McDowell began planning and preparing the Union's first deep thrust into the Old Dominion.

Elmer Ellsworth strikes a Byronic pose in 1861. "His pictures sold like wildfire," a friend wrote. "Schoolgirls dreamed over the graceful wave of his curls."

The first officer to die in the Civil War was a dashing 24-year-old colonel whose very name—Elmer E. Ellsworth—was a synonym for patriotism to millions of Northerners. In a time when virtually every town sponsored its own volunteer militia, the diminutive colonel was America's foremost parade-ground soldier and, in the popular imagination, the Union's most promising military talent.

Colonel Ellsworth had earned his reputation as commander of the U.S. Zouave Cadets (*below*), whom he had transformed from a lackadaisical group of Chicagoans into the national-champion drill team. Ellsworth modeled his unit after the exotic French Zouaves of Crimean War fame, dressing the men in baggy-trousered uniforms. He developed his own variations of the Zouave drill, featuring hundreds of swift and sometimes acrobatic maneuvers with musket and bayonet.

In the summer of 1860, with war clouds threatening to break, Ellsworth toured 20 cities in the East, challenging all comers to compete against his Zouaves. He became a celebrity overnight; editorial writers lionized him, women swooned over him, and politicians sought his friendship. Abraham Lincoln called him "the greatest little man I ever met."

Ellsworth campaigned for Lincoln during the Election of 1860. He accompanied the President-elect to Washington as his bodyguard and confidant, and became such a close family friend that he caught the measles from the Lincolns' sons Willie and Tad. When war came, Ellsworth sounded the call to arms and raised a regiment of tough volunteers from the New York City Fire Department. "They are sleeping on a volcano in Washington," he warned New York *Tribune* editor Horace Greeley on the 17th of April, 1861. "I want men who can go into a fight now."

Twelve days later, the colonel and his green regiment, called the New York Fire Zouaves, left for Washington amid great fanfare. There Ellsworth pulled political strings to guarantee that his men would be the first outfit to invade the South.

The U.S. Zouave Cadets, Colonel Ellsworth's champion drill team, perform before an audience of local militiamen in Utica, New York, in July of 1860.

Sudden Death on a Dark Staircase

James Jackson, Ellsworth's killer, was a hero to Southerners. "He was killed in defense of his home and private rights," the Confederate coroner ruled.

In the early-morning hours of May 24, 1861, the day after Virginia officially seceded from the Union, Federal troops were ordered to cross the Potomac River and seize critical points on the Virginia side. Colonel Ellsworth had wangled a choice objective for his Fire Zouaves—the port city of Alexandria. He dressed for the assault in a resplendent new uniform and pinned on his chest a gold medal that was inscribed in Latin, "Not for ourselves alone but for country."

At daybreak, a steamer put Ellsworth and his regiment ashore on an Alexandria wharf. The Union men encountered no resistance; Alexandria's only Confederate troops, a sprinkling of Virginia militia, were hurriedly leaving town. Ellsworth dispatched one company of soldiers to take the railroad station while he and a small detachment set off to capture the telegraph office. A few blocks up King Street the group came upon an inn, the Marshall House (below), which was flying a large Confederate flag. Ellsworth wanted that flag taken down immediately.

Ellsworth stationed guards in the inn and dashed upstairs with four comrades. After cutting down the flag, he started back down the stairs, preceded by Corporal Francis E. Brownell and followed by reporter Edward H. House of the New York *Tribune*. At the third-floor landing, innkeeper James W. Jackson (*left*) stood waiting with a double-barreled shotgun leveled at them. Instinctively Corporal Brownell batted the shotgun with the barrel of his musket, but the innkeeper pulled the trigger. Ellsworth was hit and, as House remembered, "He dropped forward with the heavy, horrible headlong weight which always comes with sudden death."

Jackson fired his second barrel at Brownell and missed. The corporal fired simultaneously and hit the innkeeper flush in the face. As Jackson fell dead, Brownell bayoneted the body and sent it crashing down the stairs.

Then the Union men turned to Ellsworth. He lay in a heap on the bloody Confederate flag, his gold medal driven into his chest by the shotgun blast.

The scene of Ellsworth's death, Alexandria's Marshall House, was later ransacked by souvenir hunters, who cut away the staircase where the shooting occurred.

Corporal Brownell strikes at Jackson's shotgun as Colonel Ellsworth slumps, mortally wounded. An instant later, Brownell shot Jackson through the head.

Head in hand, Lincoln and grieving officials attend Ellsworth's funeral in the East Room of the White House. On the casket lies a laurel wreath from Mrs. Lincoln.

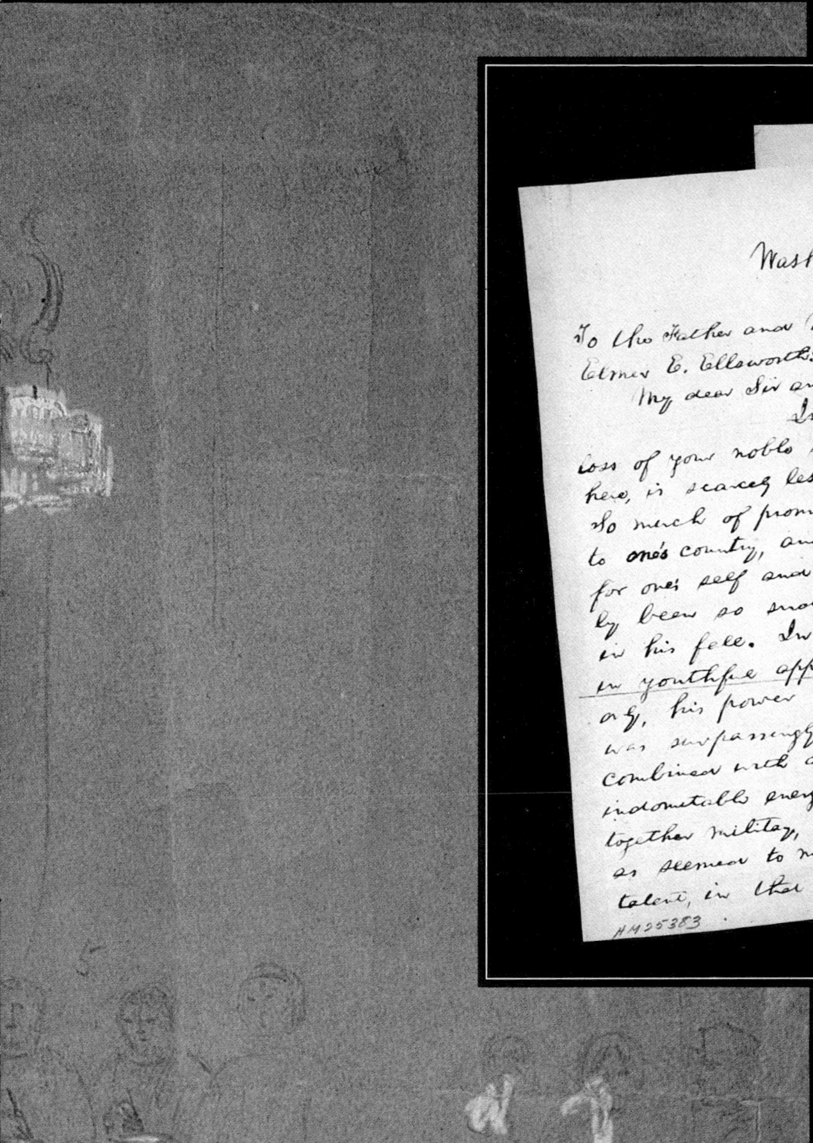

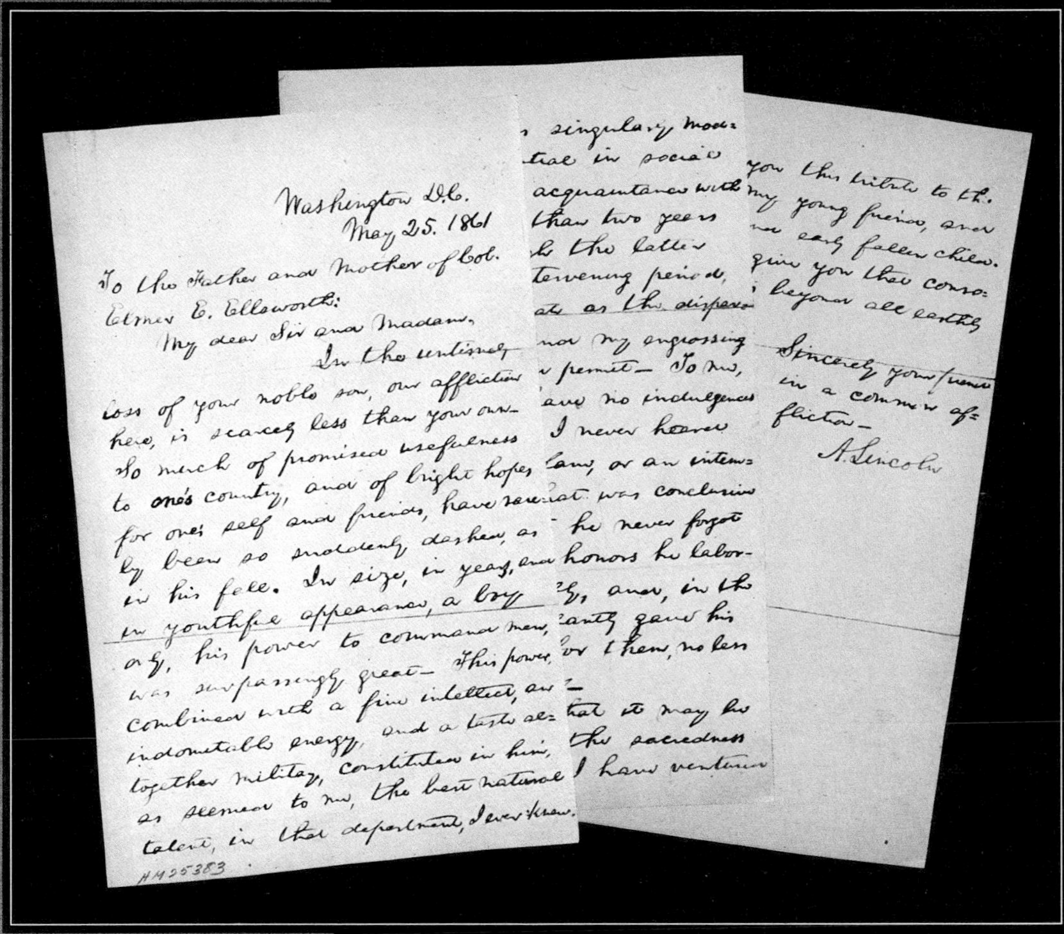

Washington D.C.
May 25. 1861

To the Father and Mother of Col.
Elmer E. Ellsworth:

My dear Sir and Madam,

In the untimely loss of your noble son, our affliction here, is scarcely less than your own. So much of promised usefulness to one's country, and of bright hopes for one's self and friends, have rarely been so suddenly dashed, as in his fall. In size, in years, and in youthful appearance, a boy only, his power to command men, was surpassingly great. This power, combined with a fine intellect, an indomitable energy, and a taste altogether military, constituted in him, as seemed to me, the best natural talent, in that department, I ever knew.

...singular... ...social acquaintance with... ...than two years... ...the latter... intervening period... ...as the dispen... ...nor my engrossing ...permit— To me, ...have no indulgence... I never heard... ...any, or an interns... ...at was conclusive he never forgot... honors he labor- ...ly, and, in th... ...antly gave his ...for them, no less ...that it may be ...the sacredness I have ventured

...you this tribute to th. ...young friend, and ...me early fallen child. ...give you this conso: ...beyond all earthly

Sincerely your friend in a common af: fliction—

A. Lincoln

A heartfelt letter from President Lincoln condoles Ellsworth's parents.

Highest Honors for the Fallen Hero

Ellsworth's death plunged the North into mourning. Bells tolled. Flags flew at half-staff. President Lincoln was grief-stricken. At the sight of his young friend's body, he sobbed, "My boy! My boy! Was it necessary that this sacrifice should be made?"

At the President's orders an honor guard brought the body to the White House, where it lay in state on May 25, 1861. A funeral ceremony followed *(left)*, attended by Cabinet members and high military officers. The casket was then moved to City Hall in New York, where thousands filed past to pay their last respects. Finally a train bore Ellsworth's remains to his hometown of Mechanicville, New York, for burial in a grave overlooking the Hudson River.

Spreading the Ellsworth Cult

The death of Elmer Ellsworth had a varied issue in the North. Sermons, editorials, songs and poems lamented his loss and proclaimed his heroism. Babies, streets, even towns were named in his honor. Corporal Brownell, the soldier who slew Ellsworth's killer, was promoted to second lieutenant in the Regular Army, and many photographs of him were sold in the small *carte de visite* format *(right)*.

From the Union's grief sprang a renewed determination. "Remember Ellsworth" became a patriotic slogan. Enlistments in the Army soared, and Zouave regiments emulating Ellsworth's cropped up everywhere. In New York, volunteers quickly filled a regiment called Ellsworth's Avengers. "We needed just such a sacrifice," thundered a minister. "Let the War go on!"

Corporal Francis E. Brownell stands on the Confederate flag that Ellsworth captured—and stained with his lifeblood.

The coat that Colonel Ellsworth was wearing when he died became a venerated relic in the North. The hole was made by the killer's shotgun slug.

COL. ELSWORTH'S LAST LETTER TO HIS PARENTS.

"Washington, May 23, 1861.

My Dear Father and Mother.—The regiment is ordered to move across the river to night. We have no means of knowing what reception we are to meet with. I am inclined to the opinion that our entrance to the city of Alexandria will be hotly contested, as I am informed a large force have arrived there to day. Should this happen, my dear parents, it may be my lot to be injured in some manner. Whatever may happen, cherish the consolation that I was engaged in the performance of a sacred duty; and to night, thinking over the probabilities of to-morrow and the occurrences of the past, I am perfectly content to accept whatever my fortune may be, confident that He who noteth even the fall of a sparrow, will have some purpose even in the fate of one like me. my darling and ever loved parents, good by. God bless protect and care for you.

"ELMER.

Memorial envelopes such as these flooded the Northern mails. The envelope at left bears a message written by Ellsworth to his parents the night before his death.

Avenge Ellsworth!
War to the knife, the knife to the hilt.

REMEMBER ELLSWORTH!

An Ellsworth portrait and scenes of his invasion of Alexandria decorate the cover of a music sheet, one of many pieces written in his praise.

Tools of the Soldier's Trade

During the first year of the War, both North and South had to use a welter of personal weapons to meet the demands of their expanding armies. Indeed, two years would pass before all the soldiers carried up-to-date firearms. However, a few models of the basic infantryman's weapon soon emerged.

Of brief but vital importance for both armies was the 1842 musket, America's first percussion musket. This weapon, the first to be truly mass-produced—manufactured with fully interchangeable parts—was slowly superseded by the 1855 rifle musket, whose rifled barrel spun the bullet and gave it greater accuracy and longer range than the ball shot from the smoothbore musket. The 1855 rifle musket served as the basis of three improved models, all of which saw extensive use during the War. A similar weapon, the imported Enfield, became the secondary rifle of both armies.

Still more advanced than the Enfield rifle and the 1855 rifle musket was the Sharps, a breech-loading rifle. Conservative ordnance officers distrusted the Sharps's intricate mechanism but, recognizing its greater rate of fire, issued it to selected companies of skirmishers. Eventually the carbine version would be heavily used by Union cavalrymen.

U.S. MODEL 1842 MUSKET
The 1842 musket weighed 10 pounds, was 57½ inches long and fired a .69-caliber round ball. Many of these weapons were converted by rifling the barrel to fire a conical bullet.

U.S. MODEL 1855 RIFLE MUSKET
The 1855 rifle musket used a Maynard percussion priming system, which had a strip of priming pellets glued between two paper tapes. But the system proved troublesome and was soon abandoned for a regular percussion cap. The weapon weighed just under 10 pounds and was 55¾ inches long.

BRITISH MODEL 1853 ENFIELD RIFLE
The standard British infantry weapon at the time of the Civil War, the Enfield rifle was widely used by both the Confederate and Union Armies. Although intended for .577-caliber ammunition, it could easily accept the .58-caliber American bullet.

SHARPS MODEL 1859 RIFLE
The Sharps rifle had a dropping breechblock, which fell when the trigger-guard lever was pulled down, exposing the bore. A .54-caliber cartridge made of linen was inserted.

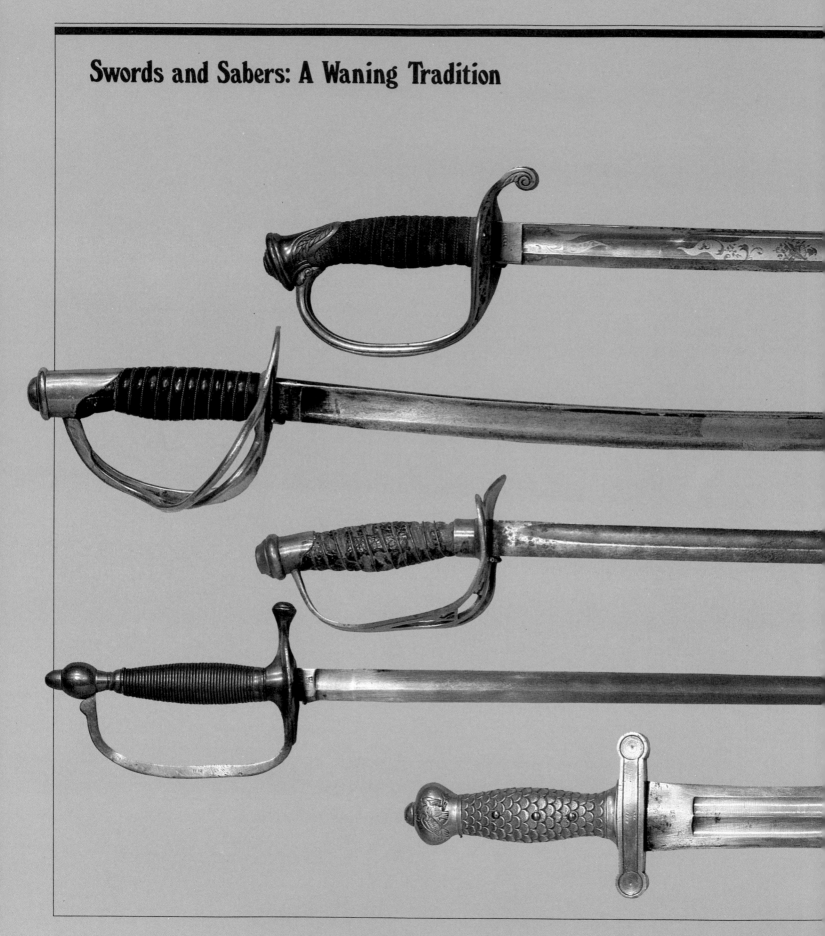

For both Union and Confederate forces, the sword served a dual purpose: It was a weapon and a symbol of rank. Infantry officers on each side wore variations of the U.S. 1850 Foot Officer's Sword but used it in combat only as a weapon of last resort. Sergeants also carried dress swords as emblems of authority.

Many cavalrymen on both sides considered the traditional saber their principal weapon, preferring it to pistols and carbines. But since cavalry charges were seldom practical in the overgrown terrain of the Eastern United States, more and more cavalrymen adopted firearms.

Gunners, whose work loading and firing cannon prevented them from carrying rifles, were often issued Roman-style short swords to defend themselves against enemy penetrations. But like their cavalry counterparts, the soldiers who manned the guns turned to revolvers in increasing numbers, and used their swords mainly as machetes.

1850 U.S. FOOT OFFICER'S SWORD
United States Army officers from the rank of second lieutenant to colonel wore the 1850 pattern sword. Many Confederate officers who had served in the prewar Army retained their U.S. swords. The hand guard and blade in this example are decorated with floral and patriotic devices.

1860 U.S. CAVALRY SABER
The 1860 saber had a curved 34-inch blade and a ridged grip for sure handling. The swept-back hand guard protected the trooper's fingers.

CONFEDERATE CAVALRY SWORD
Following a European style, this cavalry saber features a straight blade. The hand guard carries the letters *CSA* cut in brass.

U.S. NONCOMMISSIONED OFFICER'S SWORD
The sergeant's sword was elegant in design but heavy and poorly balanced. Introduced in 1840, it remained in service for 70 years.

U.S. FOOT ARTILLERY SWORD
The U.S. artilleryman's short sword was copied from the Roman-style weapon of Napoleon's gunners. A federal eagle was added to the pommel.

Horse Pistols vs. Six-shooters

Soldiers who wished to arm themselves with a handgun usually chose a revolver with rifled bore in preference to the cavalry's old smoothbore "horse pistols." The revolver was clearly superior in accuracy as well as in rate of fire and ease of loading. But selecting a revolver was complicated by the wide variety and uneven quality of the makes available.

Some gunmakers turned out single-action revolvers. These weapons were reliable but had to be cocked by a separate hand motion before each shot. Other gun manufacturers produced double-action types; pulling the trigger (or lever) cocked the gun, turned its cylinder and fired the shot. Many of these revolvers were unreliable because of faulty engineering or poor workmanship.

Both types of revolver fired much faster than the single-shot pistol, but they were just as difficult to load. Powder and bullet had to be packed into each chamber of the revolving cylinder and tamped down with a ramrod built into the weapon. This loading process would not be speeded up until self-contained metal cartridges were perfected.

COLT SECOND-MODEL DRAGOON
Weighing more than four pounds and firing a .44-caliber bullet backed by a heavy powder charge, the single-action Colt Dragoon was a formidable weapon. Its heft, however, made it difficult to manage.

WHITNEY NAVY .36
Large numbers of single-action Whitney revolvers were purchased by the U.S. Ordnance Department for standard issue and by soldiers for personal use. The term "navy" was the popular name for .36-caliber pistols, .44s being labeled "army."

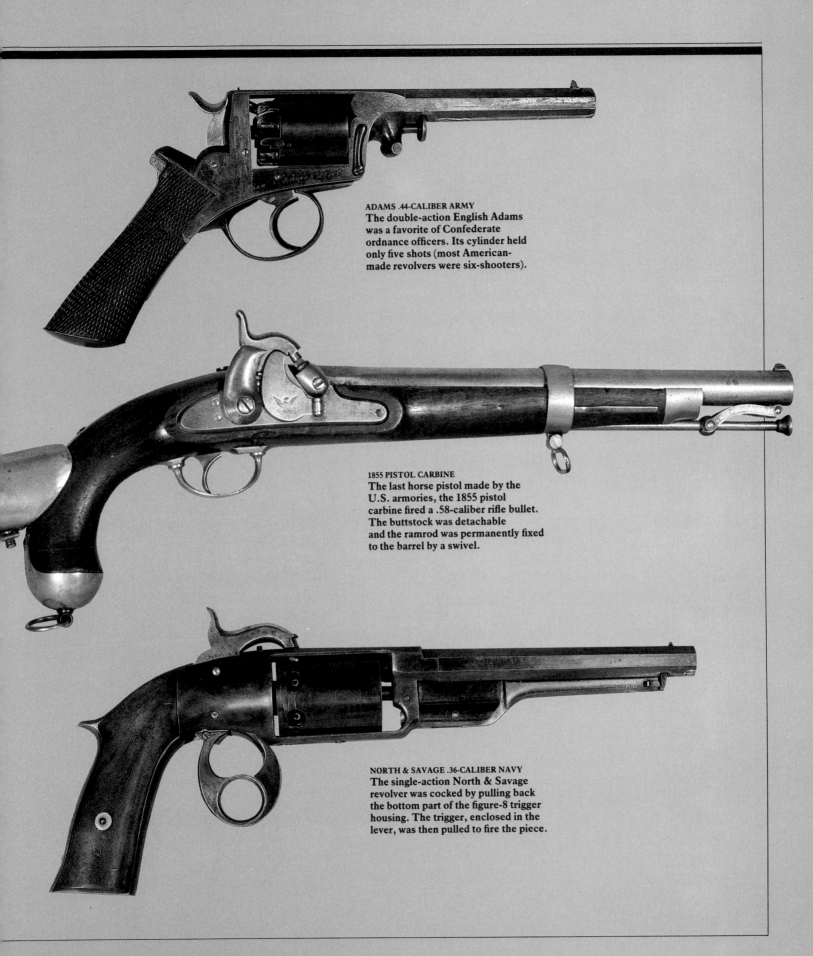

ADAMS .44-CALIBER ARMY
The double-action English Adams
was a favorite of Confederate
ordnance officers. Its cylinder held
only five shots (most American-
made revolvers were six-shooters).

1855 PISTOL CARBINE
The last horse pistol made by the
U.S. armories, the 1855 pistol
carbine fired a .58-caliber rifle bullet.
The buttstock was detachable
and the ramrod was permanently fixed
to the barrel by a swivel.

NORTH & SAVAGE .36-CALIBER NAVY
The single-action North & Savage
revolver was cocked by pulling back
the bottom part of the figure-8 trigger
housing. The trigger, enclosed in the
lever, was then pulled to fire the piece.

Action on the Flanks

"Surrounded by military preparations, with troops arriving and departing daily, with the tramp of armed men and the rapid roll of the drum ringing in my ear, I feel as if the realities of war were fast closing in on us."

LIEUTENANT COLONEL EDMUND KIRBY SMITH, C.S.A.

While preparations were under way for a large-scale confrontation in northern Virginia, soldiers and civilians on both sides learned some alarming lessons from minor actions that flared up on the flanks of the Old Dominion. Virginia presented daunting problems to defender and invader alike. In territorial extent it was the second-largest Confederate state, after Texas, and it was dangerously exposed. Invasions could come from four adjacent states: Yankee Pennsylvania and Ohio and the border states of Maryland and Kentucky. Though Virginia's northern and western borders were guarded by rivers or mountains, none of these obstacles was impassable, and in the east the state faced the Chesapeake Bay and a coastline that was much too long to be defended, or even adequately patrolled, by the craft at Confederate disposal.

In both geographic and political terms, Virginia was a fragmented state. From the Chesapeake Bay back to Richmond lay the Tidewater region. Broad rivers—the Potomac, the Rappahannock, the York and the James—ran in southeasterly courses into the bay, dividing the Tidewater into three peninsulas. The most prominent of them, framed by the York and the James and extending 60 miles west to Richmond, was so hallowed to Virginians that they called it simply the Peninsula, as though there were no other. In the Piedmont region west of Richmond the ground rose slowly to the long line of the Blue Ridge Mountains. Between

the sea and the Blue Ridge, the Virginians' ties with the South—with secession and slavery—were dominant.

Just over the Blue Ridge lay the lush, beautiful Shenandoah Valley. Walled in on the west by the jutting Allegheny Mountains, it averaged 40 miles in width and ran 125 miles southwestward from the Potomac River to Lexington, home of the Virginia Military Institute. Here the people had voted for secession, but generally with less enthusiasm than the Virginians to the east.

The Valley was vital, for the crops it produced and for its strategic position: It was a natural thoroughfare of invasion for Yankees heading south and for Confederates invading Maryland, then heading north into Pennsylvania or striking east toward Washington. East-west traffic between the midlands and the Valley was effectively blocked by the Blue Ridge except at a few gaps, the most important being Manassas Gap near the town of Front Royal, and Ashby's Gap about 20 miles north. Any army that controlled the gaps could move up or down the Valley unimpeded and probably unseen, to appear suddenly where least expected.

Beyond the Alleghenies lay a broad expanse of mountainous ridges and deep, narrow valleys that stretched west to the Ohio River and Kentucky. Northwestern Virginia, as the section was called, was a place apart, a land too hilly and rocky for large-scale farming by slave gangs. Here lived subsistence farmers who felt ignored by the

In a Northern cartoon, pro-Union western Virginia tries to stop secessionist eastern Virginia from plunging headlong into the Confederate abyss. The schism between the two parts of the state carried over into a bitter military campaign that began in May of 1861.

Statehouse in Richmond—and often were. Legislation in Richmond usually favored the large eastern slaveholders at the expense of the small western farmers, who therefore periodically threatened to go their own way. The westerners nearly rebelled in 1830, prompting Richmond to make minor concessions—such as reducing the amount of land a man must own before he was qualified to vote. But the coming of secession put the two sections once more on different roads. A majority of the Appalachian counties of northwestern Virginia voted against secession in the state referendum of May 23, and by then loyal Unionists in the east had long since met and planned to fight for the Stars and Stripes.

Clearly Virginia was vulnerable on both its flanks, and old General Winfield Scott was quite willing to probe for advantage in the east and west until his main movement matured in northern Virginia. A good base for such flank attacks was Fort Monroe, on the southern tip of the Peninsula. Fort Monroe not only threatened the Confederates with the prospect of land thrusts toward Richmond, it was a constant obstacle to Confederate traffic on the James and the York. While other coastal forts were falling to the secessionists, this one held. Behind its mammoth walls, the Federal garrison was more than secure, especially after being reinforced in early May by two regiments of Massachusetts volunteers.

The only trouble with prospective operations from Fort Monroe was the man who would command them, Benjamin Butler of Massachusetts. Scott would have preferred to appoint a more competent officer; indeed, he had angrily relieved Butler for his unauthorized occupation of Baltimore

on the 13th and 14th of May. But good fortune was running Butler's way. His performance in Baltimore was widely applauded in the North and grudgingly accepted by Lincoln, who would soon commission Butler a major general of volunteers. Secretary of War Simon Cameron and Secretary of the Treasury Salmon P. Chase were both well disposed toward Butler, and the fact that the Bay Stater was an important Democrat who wholeheartedly supported the Lincoln administration made it politic to give him a prominent command.

Scott bowed to the inevitable and put Butler in charge of the Department of Virginia and North Carolina, with headquarters at Fort Monroe. Scott even congratulated Butler for taking his new post at precisely the right time of year: "It is just the season for soft-shelled crabs, and the hogfish have just come in, and they are the most delicious pan fish you ever ate."

When Butler assumed his new command on May 22, he found barely 2,000 soldiers in the fort. But more regiments were assigned to him, and he would eventually command more than 7,500 men. He occupied the nearby town of Newport News without opposition, then began chafing under Scott's orders forbidding him to take any further action without formal permission.

Butler's willfulness soon evidenced itself again: He decided to make civil policy for President Lincoln. Three slaves belonging to a Confederate colonel escaped into Butler's lines, and the Rebel officer asked for their return. The slaves had been toiling on Confederate fortifications on the Peninsula, and Butler declined to return them to work against the Union. "I shall hold these Negroes as contraband of war," he

said; henceforth the term "contraband" was applied to increasing numbers of escaped slaves. Lincoln decided that the secession of the Southern states had abrogated the old federal Fugitive Slave Law; he accepted the general's "contraband" ruling and humorously referred to it as "Butler's fugitive slave law." This was a first step on the road to emancipation. It enabled escaped slaves to get paying jobs building Federal defenses and working as personal servants for Union officers.

While staging this political coup, Butler began considering a military move up the Peninsula from Fort Monroe. In his path

stood Bethel Church, which had given its name to two villages. Little Bethel was a few miles south of the church on the road to Newport News. Big Bethel lay on Marsh Creek, eight miles north of Fort Monroe; it was the nearest outpost of the local Confederate forces, who were headquartered 10 miles farther north at Yorktown on the York River. To Butler, the Confederates were altogether too close for comfort.

The man in command of the Southern troops on the Peninsula was a handsome, engaging, courtly and always flamboyantly attired Virginia colonel named John Bankhead Magruder. His friends called him Prince

Commanding Hampton Roads *(foreground)* and Newport News *(rear)*, Fort Monroe was a base for Union Army attacks launched up the James River toward Richmond.

John, and he did not object to it in the slightest. He was 51 years old, a West Point-trained officer who had won three commendations for bravery in Mexico.

Magruder had just 2,500 men to defend the entire Peninsula, and he deployed them as best he could. To sound an early warning and to slow any enemy advance on Yorktown, he ordered one of his newest and best regiments, the 1st North Carolina Infantry, to occupy Big Bethel. Commanding this

A political appointee, Union General Benjamin Butler often showed his resentment of West Point graduates. But he carefully concealed an unsuspected reason for his attitude: As a young man he had applied to the academy and had been rejected.

regiment was another officer of great promise, Colonel Daniel Harvey Hill. He, too, had fought with distinction in the Mexican War, but soon afterward Hill had resigned his Army commission to become a professor of mathematics at Washington College in Lexington, Virginia. When the War came he was superintendent of the North Carolina Military Institute. Hill could be troublesomely independent and was always ready to criticize his superiors. But he had an instinct for a fight.

Hill and his Tarheels reached Big Bethel on June 7. They spent all of that day and the next one erecting earthworks and felling trees to build defenses on both sides of the Back River (*page 83*), which was crossed by a bridge that carried the road from Fort Monroe to Yorktown. On their left lay a marsh that would impede infantry movement, so Hill stationed merely a handful of sharpshooters there. To the right, on some high ground behind a cluster of buildings, the Confederates emplaced a cannon of the Richmond Howitzers and 208 men of the 3rd Virginia Infantry.

North of the river, the main defense line was held by the 1st North Carolina and the remaining four guns of the Richmond Howitzers. If the Yankees from Fort Monroe did not come across the bridge, they might ford the river east of the bridge, on the far side of the swamp. To guard against this move, the Confederates built more earthworks. Hill had to stretch his 1,400 troops thin to man all the defenses, but the construction work was finished by June 9. Early the following morning word came that a Union column was approaching.

Butler had learned of Hill's occupation of Big Bethel, and he had decided to drive the

Confederates out, thus preventing any raid on Federal outposts near Fort Monroe and Newport News. The general's plan, which he had devised without bothering to consult Scott as ordered, called for two columns to move independently toward Big Bethel and then converge for a surprise attack at dawn. One column incorporated the 5th New York, Duryée's colorful Zouaves and the 3rd New York Regiment. The other column comprised the 7th New York and parts of the 1st Vermont and 4th Massachusetts. The 1st and 2nd New York Regiments were readied to reinforce the attackers, if needed. Butler assigned the task of leading the attack to another Massachusetts militiaman, Brigadier General Ebenezer Pierce.

The Federals, about 4,400 strong, moved out before 1 a.m. on June 10, and General Pierce soon learned how difficult it was for unskilled troops and neophyte leaders to make coordinated movements in the dark. On Butler's orders, the Zouaves had tied their white turbans around their arms, while the other soldiers wrapped their arms with white cloths, all so that they would recognize one another as friends in the dark. The precaution did no good, however. As the two columns converged below Little Bethel, they mistook each other for the enemy and opened fire. Twenty-one soldiers were killed or wounded before the firing stopped, and by then the Confederates were thoroughly prepared to give them a hot welcome. Pierce patiently listened to Colonel Abram Duryée, commander of the Zouave regiment named after him, who argued that it was madness to continue now that they had been discovered. But Pierce decided to go ahead with the attack anyway.

It was about 8 a.m. when Yankee skirmishers met and drove in Hill's pickets south of Big Bethel. As they approached the first Confederate earthworks, some of the Federals were surprised and annoyed to find that Hill's men were not standing out in open fields in the standard line of battle, offering them good targets. "They were completely in ambush," complained a New York soldier, "and within the embankment of one of the strongest fortifications in this section of the country."

The Confederates braced to meet the attack. At 9:15 the main body of the enemy came in sight, and the Richmond Howitzers, under the command of Captain George Wythe Randolph, opened fire.

Lieutenant Benjamin Huske of the 1st North Carolina reported that the first Confederate fire shook up the Federal infantrymen and forced them "to do some pretty scientific dodging." The Yankee soldiers conceded that point. "Their batteries," a Zouave wrote later, "received us warmly"; cannonballs "whistled through the air and bushes as if they meant something nasty."

Pierce's artillery opened up in return, firing ineffectually. Pierce deployed his men in line of battle along the woods on both sides of the road. Units on his extreme right and left began spreading outward in an attempt to turn the flanks of the Confederates. Duryée and part of his regiment moved off to the right, skirting the marshy ground in hopes of crossing the creek at a ford and getting behind Hill. The detachment soon ran into heavy fire. "At one time it seemed as if the balls could never come so thick and fast," wrote one of the Zouaves. "At every boom of the cannon we would drop flat on our faces and rise instantly, but they came so fast after that that many of us

"Contraband" Slaves at Work in Fort Freedom

The slaves in Virginia's Tidewater region were quick to learn by the grapevine that General Benjamin Butler, the Union commander at Fort Monroe, had refused to return three escaped slaves to their Confederate owner on the ground that such valuable workmen were legitimate "contraband of war." Immediately, scores of slaves began fleeing their masters to seek haven within the Union lines around Fort Monroe and Newport News. They traveled by river and creek, using old scows, oyster boats and dugout canoes, leaving no trails for men or bloodhounds. On the 27th of May, 1861, only three days after Butler's contraband ruling, the general had 67 fugitives on his hands. By the end of July, just two months later, some 900 men, women and children had sought refuge in Fort Monroe, which the slaves had renamed "the freedom fort."

At the fort, the men were put to work at a variety of tasks by the general's quartermaster. Most of them were assigned to heavy work, such as unloading supply vessels or building a series of earthwork bastions to guard the neck of land that led to the fort. Some became officer's servants (*below*). A few acted as scouts for the Army, guiding patrols through the area's swamps and forests. The men were paid modest wages, from which small sums were deducted for the upkeep of their dependents.

General Butler started a school with day classes for the children and night sessions for the adults. Many of the refugee families built their own houses in the nearby ruins of the town of Hampton, which had been burned by the Confederates to deprive the Federal troops of its conveniences. The new town was well laid out, although it had one odd feature: In the heart of a wartime Southern community, the streets bore such names as Lincoln and Union.

Escaped slaves serve an officers' mess of Duryée's Zouaves at Fort Monroe in 1861. At center sits lanky Adjutant Joseph Hamblin, later a general.

did not take the trouble." All along the line, men were frightened or bewildered by their initial battle. "It was a grand and awful scene," wrote another, "but I did not realize it fully until it was over."

Thwarted on his right, Pierce tried advancing with his left-flank units, Colonel Frederick Townsend's 3rd New York and a few companies of the 5th New York. Unfortunately for the Federals, a wooded ravine had separated one of Townsend's companies from the rest of his line during the advance. When Townsend's men looked beyond the ravine and saw their lost company, they mistook it for the enemy and opened fire. Then, fearing that their flank had been turned, they hastily withdrew.

With this thrust foiled, Pierce saw no alternative but to try once more to push his way around the enemy's left flank. Major Theodore Winthrop, General Butler's military secretary, led forward a group of companies from the 1st Vermont and the 4th Massachusetts. They went through and around the marshy ground, pushed their way across a ford, and advanced against a Confederate strong point that was bolstered with a howitzer. Winthrop, hoping to find a chink in the earthworks through which he could lead a charge on the pestiferous cannon, climbed a fence and waved his sword, gesturing his men onward. "Rally, boys, rally!" he shouted. "Come on, boys; one charge, and the day is ours!"

Those were Winthrop's last words. A Confederate bullet struck him square in the chest and went all the way through his body. Major Winthrop died instantly, and his assault died with him. "He was the only one of the enemy," Colonel Hill wrote later, "who exhibited even an approxi-

mation to courage during the whole day."

Pierce's force was in disarray now. Many of the men, a soldier later wrote, "scattered singly and in groups, without form or organization, looking far more like men enjoying a huge picnic than soldiers awaiting a battle." After barely two hours of fighting, Pierce decided to halt the action and return to Fort Monroe. The retreat was just as confused as the assault had been. But the Yankees were not pursued, and they managed to retire safely to Hampton.

Behind them lay the War's first scene of post-battle horror. Some five dozen soldiers, all but 10 of them Yankees, lay wounded,

A storytelling Confederate map traces the course of the Rebel victory at Big Bethel on June 10, 1861. The Confederates emplaced most of their howitzers behind earthworks on the Back River's north side *(bottom)*. As Union regiments advanced from the south *(top)*, they were slowed down by the marshy riverside terrain and repulsed by Confederate fire.

Colonel John Bankhead Magruder, the Confederate commander at Big Bethel, was much admired as a bon vivant. He displayed, a fellow officer said, "princely hospitality" and "the taste of a connoisseur," and was "always ready to participate in the amusements of his subalterns."

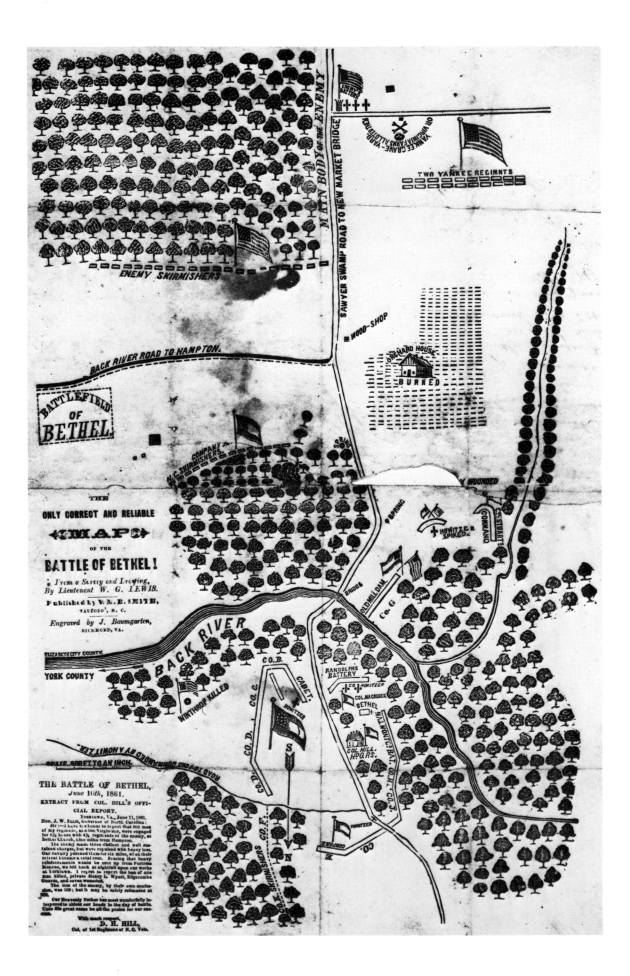

writing and shrieking in pain. "One brave boy with his arm torn off cried out to his comrades to avenge him," wrote a Zouave. Another youngster showed a hand dangling from a shred of flesh and begged someone to cut it off "as the pain was dreadful." Cried Lieutenant Huske, "Great God in mercy, avert the awful results of civil war!" Yet the Federals managed to salvage some pride from their defeat. "I have seen enough to satisfy me first, that war ain't play," wrote a Zouave, "and second, that our regiment ain't got no cowards in it."

For all that, it was not much of a battle. The Confederates lost just one man killed, while the Yankees counted 18 dead. The basic situation at the end of the Peninsula had changed not at all. But the little struggle did have noteworthy results. Prince John Magruder and his field commander Hill were made generals, and Pierce lost his command. When the War Department refused to confirm his rank, Pierce enlisted as a private.

As for General Butler, he was roundly blamed for the defeat by his officers and the people at home. One of Duryée's men declared bitterly that if any good came from the defeat, then "we earnestly hope it may be the means of removing our New York troops at least from Massachusetts generals, who have been fledged in the foul nest of party politics, without the least military merit." He prophesied that "if such generalship is to be continued, it will doom thousands to an untimely end." Benjamin Butler was one general who would make other costly blunders.

Even as the Northerners met with defeat on the Peninsula, Federal troops on Virginia's other flank were winning the Union's first faint victory. At stake was the future of all

of western Virginia, and considerably more.

From the outset, this rugged region had been a bright hope for the Federals. On May 13 a convention met in Wheeling to discuss seceding from Virginia and joining the Union. "Let the world see," the Wheeling *Intelligencer* urged its readers, "that there was one green spot where unyielding patriotism rallied." But while the radicals for their part talked of forming a new state, conserva-

Zouaves of the 5th New York make a desperate charge on a Confederate battery at Big Bethel. Six Zouaves died in the vain assault, and their garish uniforms, a Confederate said, "contrasted greatly with the pale, fixed faces of their dead owners."

Northern troops needed to take possession of the territory if they were to guard the vital Baltimore & Ohio Railroad, which ran through the area and connected Harpers Ferry with the Ohio River. The railroad was a life line for bringing troops and supplies from the western states.

Luckily, Lincoln had exactly the right man for the job. The officer was Major General George B. McClellan, commanding the Department of the Ohio, and he did not wait to be ordered into western Virginia. Learning on May 26 that secessionists were moving to burn the bridges of the Baltimore & Ohio line, McClellan sent two columns into action. One, led by Colonel Benjamin Kelley, moved south from Wheeling toward Grafton, repairing the damaged bridges as it went. Brigadier General Thomas Morris led the other column across the Ohio River at Parkersburg and drove eastward to link up with Kelley. With good fortune, they would converge at Grafton, catching the Confederates between them.

Their quarry was Colonel George A. Porterfield, who faced a far worse situation than McClellan could have hoped. Governor John Letcher of Virginia had assigned Porterfield to command the state troops at Grafton, where the northwestern Virginia railroad joined the B & O route to Parkersburg. Although Porterfield could severely hamper Yankee communications by holding the Grafton junction, Richmond had given him precious little to work with. He had only 1,500 troops, and they were dismayingly undisciplined, with some companies seeming to wander in and out of camp at will. By June 2, Porterfield had just 773 men on active duty, and he had fallen back to Philippi, a tiny village a few miles south of Grafton.

tives argued that they had been the true representatives of Virginia ever since the Richmond government seceded, and that they should establish a provisional government for the whole of the Old Dominion. So another convention was called for June 11 in hopes of settling the matter.

President Lincoln welcomed the western Virginians' political initiatives. But the first order of business was purely military: The

That day Porterfield received word that Colonel Kelley was coming, and that General Morris was believed to be only 20 miles northwest of him. In fact, the two Yankee columns had already joined forces in Grafton, not that it would have made any difference to Porterfield. The knowledge that his foe numbered at least 3,000 was quite enough; he had to leave Philippi—and with unbecoming haste.

Loading his few wagons with what they could carry, Porterfield assembled his officers that evening and announced that if they were attacked, they would retire toward Beverly, about 40 miles south, where he expected to find reinforcements. It was a rainy night, uncomfortable for all. One of his captains looked out the headquarters window in the Barbour House, Philippi's only hotel, and exclaimed, "Hell, any army marching tonight must be made up of a set of damned fools!" Porterfield apparently agreed, for he let his officers sleep the night away; no one knew that the Confederate outpost guards had left their posts without permission or replacement and had come into town seeking shelter. Philippi was entirely unguarded, and plenty of "damned fool" Yankees were marching through the night, bent on attack.

The Federals struck at daybreak, opening fire with two artillery pieces. The Confederates were taken completely by surprise. In a little while Porterfield recovered from the shock, and did a creditable job of organizing his men and hustling them out of Philippi on the road to Beverly.

One of the last men to flee the town was Private John Sheffee, a member of a Highland County company of Virginians. Looking behind him, Sheffee saw a mounted Yankee riding toward him, took aim with his

Killed by a shell fragment, Federal Lieutenant John T. Greble topples backward from his cannon at Big Bethel. Troops of the 2nd New York, rushing up at right, withdrew with the gun and Greble's body as the clash turned into a Union rout.

pistol and felled the horseman. "Sergeant, I have done it!" he shrieked in joy.

"Done what?" the sergeant asked.

"I flopped that big fellow from his horse that was coming after us so savage." Sheffee had wounded Colonel Kelley, and he would be captured for his trouble. Nevertheless Kelley's fall halted the Federals' pursuit, and the fleeing Confederates reached Beverly safely and kept on going.

The whole affair was even less significant than the fight at Big Bethel. But on June 3, 1861, the Union press crowed about an enemy rout and referred to it as the "Philippi Races." "The chivalry couldn't stand" said the Wheeling *Intelligencer*, revealing the mountaineers' resentment of the elitist pretensions of Tidewater Virginians. "They scattered like rats from a burning barn."

McClellan, who had been absent from the scene during the fight, chose not to follow up his victory with pursuit. Rather, he spent the next few weeks vigorously training more troops in Ohio, and for good reason. The 90-day enlistments of many of his Ohio regiments were due to expire in the middle of July, and he wanted to use those troops before he lost them. Besides, there were renewed Confederate threats to the B & O line. And then came news of an enemy build-up at Beverly.

This Confederate activity was the work of a new commander. Colonel Porterfield had been relieved with a mild reprimand and replaced by Brigadier General Robert Selden Garnett, a 41-year-old Virginian who had served with gallantry in Mexico. Garnett was known as a strict disciplinarian and one of the brightest officers in the old Regular Army. But he was a man shaken by the loss of his beloved wife and child, who had died of illness in Washington Territory. In accepting his western Virginia assignment, he turned morbid, telling several friends that he was going to his death.

Garnett quickly immersed himself in the work of training and organizing his forces just west of the town of Beverly. Here he was close enough to provide at least a threat to the B & O, and at the same time he stood in the way of any Federal attempt to penetrate deeper into the state or toward the Shenandoah. By early July, Garnett had built his army to about 6,000. He put the bulk of the troops on Laurel Mountain; the rest, about 1,300, he placed on nearby Rich Mountain. Garnett assigned the command of the Rich Mountain units to the handsome Lieutenant Colonel John Pegram, a 29-year-old West Pointer whose only real service thus far had been on the frontier. Garnett made his own headquarters on Laurel Mountain and waited for the enemy.

In response to Garnett's moves, McClellan himself took the field. On the 21st of June he marched his fresh regiments into western Virginia and moved to link up with the bulk of his army, which was already garrisoning the Grafton-Philippi area. "Bear in mind that you are in the country of friends," he admonished his soldiers, "that you are here to protect, not to destroy." He feared that any acts of casual plunder would stir up the secessionist minority in the region and upset the cautious politics of Lincoln and Francis H. Pierpont, whom the second political convention at Wheeling had just elected provisional governor of a pro-Union rival to the Richmond government.

McClellan brought to bear 16 Ohio regiments, nine from Indiana, two raised in Wheeling, two troops of cavalry and 24 fieldpieces in four batteries. In all, his army numbered some 20,000 men. About 5,400 were assigned in detachments to guard the line of the Baltimore & Ohio. General Morris commanded a brigade at Philippi, and he was getting nervous about Garnett's growing forces. Three Union brigades were assembled around Grafton, and these McClellan assigned to three new brigade commanders: Brigadier General Newton Schleich, Colonel Robert L. McCook and Brigadier General William S. Rosecrans.

Although none of the three officers was considered especially promising, Rosecrans had a fair amount of experience. A West Point graduate, he had missed the Mexican War and spent most of his service in unglamorous engineering pursuits until he resigned his commission in 1854. When the War came, he was managing a nearly bankrupt kerosene factory. McClellan, needing professionally trained officers in a hurry, appointed him as an aide on his staff, and soon thereafter the War Department made Rosecrans a brigadier general, probably because of his energy in arming and training Ohio volunteers.

Paying due heed to the inexperience of his officers and men, McClellan planned his campaign carefully. He declared that "no prospect of a brilliant victory shall induce me to depart from my intention of gaining success by maneuvering rather than by fighting"; he simply would not send these "raw men of mine" into real battle if he could avoid it. According to his plan, two columns would advance at the same time. Morris would move to Laurel Mountain and keep Garnett occupied with demonstrations; meanwhile, McClellan would lead the other three brigades against Rich Mountain and

George B. McClellan, the rising young Union general, was renowned as the designer of a simpler, less costly cavalry saddle. The McClellan saddle was adopted by the War Department in 1859 and was used by both sides throughout the War.

Pursuing the routed Confederates, Union troops hurry down the main street of Philippi, Virginia, on June 3, 1861. According to the *Harper's* artist who sketched the scene, the Confederate flag atop the hotel (*center*) was soon "carried away" by a cannonball, and "the Union flag is now floating in its place."

what was mistakenly believed to be the main enemy force. McClellan planned to circle behind Pegram's left flank, cutting off his retreat. It was a tactic that had been used with some success by Scott at Cerro Gordo in the Mexican War, and McClellan was not above a bit of flattery in declaring that he would emulate the master.

McClellan cautiously put his plan into operation. Heading south from Grafton on June 30, he marched 25 miles in three days, reaching Buckhannon, about 10 miles from Garnett's position, on July 2. Three days later and still en route to Rich Mountain, he wrote the War Department: "The delays I have met have been irksome to me in the extreme, but I feel that it would be exceedingly foolish to give way to impatience and advance before everything is prepared."

McClellan finally reached his destination on July 10. By then Morris and his column had arrived in front of Laurel Mountain and had begun skirmishing with Garnett. Stiff resistance had convinced Morris that the real Confederate strength lay in his front, rather than on Rich Mountain, but he could not persuade McClellan to accept that fact. Nevertheless, the Confederate defenses on Rich Mountain were formidable, and McClellan decided to precede a ground attack with an artillery bombardment.

General Rosecrans unexpectedly showed a good bit of dash. A Union sympathizer named David Hart came into his lines that evening and said he knew a way to flank Pegram's position. Rosecrans quickly incorporated Hart's route in a plan for turning Pegram's flank. McClellan agreed to

Outnumbered Confederates on Rich Mountain (*left*) make a doomed stand against the attack force of Brigadier General William S. Rosecrans on the 11th of July, 1861. Rosecrans later confided to his wife: "If the enemy had disciplined troops and any enterprise, how they would have stirred us up."

the scheme, though apparently with reluctance. The general undoubtedly disliked the risk of sending a large detachment of inexperienced men through rugged terrain in the early-morning darkness. But the sally promised great things if successful, and that made the risk worth taking. Rosecrans was to move out at 4 a.m.

With Hart in the lead, the attack force of 1,900-odd men swung silently around the southern spur of Rich Mountain, out of Pegram's sight. In spite of rain, dim light and the rough terrain, Rosecrans pushed the men on without stopping. It was just as well, for the Confederates captured a Union sergeant who revealed to Pegram that a flanking movement was under way. Pegram's trouble was that he could not learn from the sergeant

which flank was being turned. Erroneously guessing that the threat was to his right, on the northern summit of Rich Mountain, Pegram moved most of his small command there. He was so confident of his men that he even sent word to Garnett suggesting that he attack McClellan.

Despite the long march, and despite getting lost at least once, Rosecrans and his column finally clambered up the back slope of the mountain some time after noon on the 11th of July and drove toward the rear of the enemy, whom they outnumbered by about 6 to 1. Skirmishing began around 2 p.m., and half an hour later the Federal troops launched their first attack. At the last moment, Confederate gunners turned their one small fieldpiece on Rosecrans, and the

Confederate Brigadier General
Robert Selden Garnett, killed during
his retreat from Laurel Mountain,
was the first Civil War general to die
in action. In deference to Garnett's
heroism during the Mexican War, a
Union honor guard conveyed the
body to his family under a truce flag.

infantrymen ran to their crude breastworks and opened fire.

David Hart suddenly found himself in the middle of a small battle right on his own father's farm. "The rain began pouring down in torrents," he reported a few days later, "while the enemy fired his cannon, cutting off the tree tops over our heads quite lively." It seemed to Hart that Pegram had 25 or 30 cannon instead of one. For 30 minutes the Federals stood firm under the Confederate volleys, then two regiments went off to the left through bushes that Hart said were "so thick we could not see out, nor could the enemy see us." The rest of Rosecrans' force attempted to storm the Rebel works; failing, they took cover behind rocks and logs.

Pegram's men, believing the enemy was in flight, rose from their rifle pits in a cheering pursuit. At that, said Hart, "Our boys lit into them with their Enfield and Minié rifles, and I never heard such screaming in my life." The Yankees shot down the Confederate artillery horses, felled most of the gunners and wounded Garnett's chief of artillery. The regiments off in the bush joined in with a volley, and all of the Federals rushed forward in a countercharge. "The whole earth seemed to shake," said Hart.

After three hours of fighting, the defenders retreated down the mountain toward the northeast. With the much larger forces of McClellan in his front and Rosecrans now on his flank and rear, Pegram had no choice but to abandon the rest of his works on the northern crest of Rich Mountain and try to join Garnett.

Through it all, McClellan made no move to join the battle himself, much to the dismay of some of his officers, who felt that the gen-

eral should take decisive action. On hearing the opening volley of Rosecrans' attack, many of McClellan's Ohio boys jumped up, expecting to be ordered to attack and thus crush the Confederates between two fires. But McClellan simply rode to his front line and sat listening intently, tracking Rosecrans' movement by the sound of the advancing gunfire. It seemed that Rosecrans had matters well in hand.

Now Pegram was on the run in an attempt to save what remained of his command. Late that day about half of his Confederates escaped from Rosecrans and made their way to Beverly. Pegram and the rest wandered all through the day and the night that followed, trying to find a route through the wild country to join Garnett, who was north of them on Laurel Mountain. Late on July 12, exhausted and famished after going for two days without food, Pegram's force finally offered to surrender. When McClellan accepted the next morning, Pegram came into the Union lines with 555 officers and men.

All the while, Garnett's position grew steadily more desperate. Once he learned of Rosecrans' success, the Confederate general decided that he would have to abandon Laurel Mountain. With Rosecrans drawing dangerously near the Beverly road, Garnett moved away to the northeast, pursued closely by Morris and his brigade. The Federals chased him throughout July 12, and the next day they caught up with the Confederate rear guard at Carrick's Ford on the Cheat River, 30 miles from Rich Mountain. By then several hundred of Garnett's soldiers were missing—lost, deserted, or captured on the retreat.

Garnett pressed on. The tail of his column had just crossed the Cheat at Carrick's Ford when he learned that Morris was approaching rapidly. Garnett sent ahead for reinforcements, then began positioning the one available company to resist the Yankee crossing.

At the first enemy fire from across the Cheat, Garnett's aide ducked. The general told him that one could never duck in time. A moment later the officer heard a bullet strike something soft and turned to see Garnett sprawled on the ground. The gener-

Pro-Union men from western Virginia, eager to fight the secessionist Richmond government, form ranks in Morgantown to enlist in the Union Army in the summer of 1861. By the end of the year, the anti-Richmond "Reorganized Government of Virginia" had supplied the Union 12,688 soldiers.

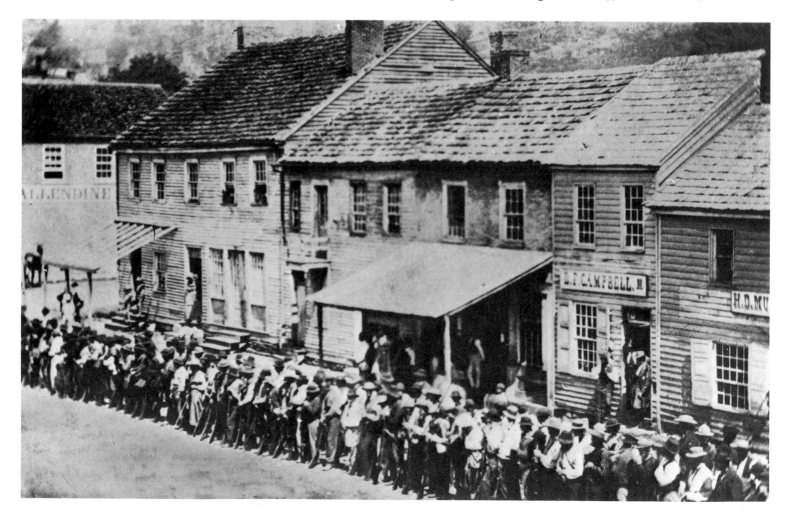

al's presentiment of death had come true.

It did not take long for the Federal troops to rout the Rebel rear guard. Colonel Ebenezer Dumont of the 7th Indiana was one of the first Union officers to cross the river, and he immediately found the body of Garnett, who had been his comrade in arms in Mexico. Dumont raised his hands in anguish over his fallen friend and exclaimed, "Poor Bob Garnett!"

The fighting had no sooner stopped than McClellan began touting his triumph: In his reports to Washington he understated Rosecrans' role, giving the impression that the flanking movement was his own conception. Nevertheless, McClellan had acquitted himself well. He had boldly insisted on invading western Virginia, had conducted a successful campaign there, had ensured the region's entry into the Union as a state in 1863 and had, in the process, made it strategically impossible for the slave state of Kentucky to join the Confederacy. The people of the North, hungering for heroes and succcsses, quite naturally hailed McClellan as "the Young Napoleon" and, in an affectionate reference to his stature, "Little Mac." General Scott sent warm congratulations: "The general in chief, and what is more, the Cabinet, including the President, are charmed with your activity, valor and consequent successes." Clearly McClellan was destined for greater things.

During the fighting in western Virginia, everything had been quiet in the Shenandoah Valley. After seizing Harpers Ferry on April 18 and thus closing the northern gateway to the Valley, the Virginians had begun building an army to defend the Valley. The organization and training of the army was turned over to a professor from the Virginia Military Institute who was so eccentric and erratic that some considered him insane. Colonel Thomas Jonathan Jackson took charge on the 29th of April and applied himself zealously to the task. Only two weeks later he was superseded by Confederate General Joseph E. Johnston, another Virginian, but one as distinguished as the professor was obscure.

Johnston had attended West Point with Robert E. Lee, had fought the Seminoles and the Mexicans and had won repeated commendation. When he resigned his commission as a brigadier general in the Regular Army to side with Virginia, he became a major general of state troops, ranking second only to Lee. Then, when the Virginia army was absorbed by the Confederacy, President Davis made Johnston one of his first brigadier generals. Everyone expected much from the 54-year-old officer. So did he.

Johnston continued the task of building an army. Within two months he had organized four brigades, each with a battery of artillery and all sharing the services of the 1st Virginia Cavalry, commanded by Colonel J.E.B. (Jeb) Stuart. This was Johnston's Army of the Shenandoah, numbering more than 10,000 men.

By the time his army was substantially complete, Johnston had changed his base of operations. He had never deemed Harpers Ferry defensible, and had spent more than a month persuading Richmond to allow him to pull his army south toward Winchester. He had received reports that a Yankee army of 18,000 men was poised and ready to march against him, and he regarded Winchester as a much better place to defend, since it controlled all the main roads into the Valley

The hillside town of Harpers Ferry, Virginia, lay heavily damaged when Union troops occupied it in July 1861. The retreating Confederates had stripped the riverside arsenal and the munitions factories, and they had blown up the railroad bridge across the Potomac River.

and also the vital Manassas Gap Railroad to the east. So Johnston occupied the Winchester area and waited there confidently for the enemy advance.

The Union army Johnston expected was being marshaled in Chambersburg, Pennsylvania, expressly for the task of keeping him busy and preventing him from moving east on the Manassas Gap Railroad to reinforce the Confederate army gathering in northern Virginia. But the Chambersburg force appeared to be immobilized by an endless chain of real and imaginary problems. To begin with, Winfield Scott had severely damaged the army's chances of success by sending his longtime friend, Major General Robert Patterson, to take command. Patterson was simply too old, slow and timid to handle an active field command, and he virtually conceded as much in early messages to Scott. Announcing that he intended to take Harpers Ferry, Patterson said that he would try to "threaten" Johnston out of his position, and if that failed, he would circle the enemy's flank and advance, "however slowly," on Winchester.

After two weeks of sluggish preparation, Patterson on June 15 began to march on Harpers Ferry. He arrived there well after Johnston had evacuated to Winchester. Elated at his bloodless victory, Patterson wired Scott that now he intended to march on Winchester "and recover, without a struggle, a conquered country." But when rumors came into Harpers Ferry that Johnston had turned around and was advancing, Patterson at once abandoned his prize and returned to safety north of the Potomac. Johnston's force had not left its Winchester camps. But it soon would.

The Innocent, Cocky Volunteers

The fresh-faced young men who rushed to arms in the spring of 1861 were marked by a special innocence and fervor: They did not know, as later volunteers would, what lay ahead. They would find out only at their own great cost.

Those first volunteers for the Union and the Confederacy were ill-prepared for war in almost every way. The overwhelming majority had no military experience and little training; the most experienced of them were cadets from military schools and parade soldiers from state militia units. Many lacked weapons of any sort. For months, many lacked standard uniforms; their motley garb identifies several of the portraits on these pages as early War photographs. Among the Northern troops, the Garibaldi Guards (*right*) and other foreign-speaking units could barely understand an order in English. And the men on both sides often followed a democratic practice that would get many of them killed: They elected their own company officers. "The question of military fitness," a Union general wrote, "was about the last one asked."

Yet with little to recommend their prospects for survival, both sides expected to win a quick victory and confidently disparaged the enemy's fighting ability. Southerners claimed that any one of them equaled five Northerners. "Just throw three or four shells among those blue-bellied Yankees and they'll scatter like sheep," a North Carolinian bragged. Such boasting prompted an Indiana farm boy to say, "Those fellers down South are just big bluffers. They would rather talk than fight."

COLONEL FREDERIC D'UTASSY (*CENTER*) AND MEN OF THE GARIBALDI GUARDS, NEW YORK

UNKNOWN ENLISTED MAN, NEW ENGLAND MILITIA

DRUM MAJOR C.R.M. POHLÉ, 1ST VIRGINIA INFANTRY

WILLIAM B. OTT, 4TH VIRGINIA INFANTRY; KILLED AT BULL RUN

UNKNOWN UNION ZOUAVE

JAMES G. BARKER, NORWICH UNIVERSITY CADETS

WILLIAM OVERTON, VIRGINIA MILITARY INSTITUTE

UNKNOWN ENLISTED MEN, SUSSEX LIGHT DRAGOONS, VIRGINIA STATE CAVALRY

UNKNOWN SOLDIERS, NEW HAMPSHIRE VOLUNTEERS

UNKNOWN CONFEDERATE PRIVATE

UNKNOWN UNION ARTILLERYMAN

FIRST LIEUTENANT EDWARD K. BUTLER, 69TH NEW YORK STATE MILITIA

FIRST LIEUTENANT THOMAS M. LOGAN, HAMPTON LEGION, SOUTH CAROLINA VOLUNTEERS

The Battle Is Joined

"The enemy has assailed my outposts in heavy force. I have fallen back on the line of Bull Run and will make a stand at Mitchell's Ford."

GENERAL P.G.T. BEAUREGARD, JULY 17, 1861

General Irvin McDowell was a mass of paradoxes. He abstained from alcohol, tobacco, coffee and tea, but was a ravening glutton. ("He was such a gargantuan feeder," an officer wrote of his first supper with McDowell, "and so absorbed in the dishes before him that he had little time for conversation"; the general finished off the huge repast with a whole watermelon, which he pronounced "monstrous fine.") McDowell had won promotion for gallant service in Mexico, but his demeanor did him no good as the commanding officer of the Union Army in northern Virginia: He could not remember faces or names, he was a poor listener, and he treated his subordinates with a brusque indifference that lost him their professional respect and even their good will.

Such was Irvin McDowell's saddest paradox: He alienated the only men who could help him at a time when he needed all the help he could get. For in July of 1861 the general was a desperate man, under relentless pressure to attack the enemy with an army that was conspicuously unready. All too many of his officers were either inactive old veterans or inexperienced youths. His enlisted men were short on weapons, ammunition and equipment. He had no reliable maps of the difficult terrain of northern Virginia, and he lacked enough cavalry to provide the detailed information required for drawing adequate maps. And though McDowell's troops had been drilling for weeks, their training was far from complete.

To cure these ills, McDowell needed the one thing he could not have: "I wanted very much a little time," he said, "an opportunity to test my machinery, to move it around and see whether it worked smoothly or not."

McDowell's superior, General Winfield Scott, would gladly have given him the time he craved; Scott, too, had been reluctant to mount a campaign in northern Virginia, preferring his slower and less bloody plan to strangle the Confederacy by blockading the seacoast and controlling the Mississippi. But the decision was not Scott's to make; it was Lincoln's, and the President himself had been constantly exhorted to attack by the Northern press and public, which fumed and fretted over the presence of a Rebel army at the very doorstep of the nation's capital. After the Federal defeat at Big Bethel on June 10, the President had finally run out of patience. He ordered Scott to mount a campaign in northern Virginia, and Scott reluctantly ordered McDowell to devise a plan of attack. McDowell protested to Scott that his army was inexperienced, but the general only replied, "You are green, it is true, but they are green also; you are all green alike."

McDowell had worked up several plans of attack before one was accepted by Scott, Lincoln and the President's Cabinet. The Federal army, dividing into three columns to increase its pace and mobility, would advance westward on roughly parallel routes, seizing the Confederate outposts at Fairfax Court House, 16 miles from Washington, and at Centreville, five miles beyond. At this stage, two of the columns would push ahead and make a diversionary attack on the likely center of the Confederate line at Bull Run. The third column would skirt the Confederates' right flank and strike southward, cutting the railroad to Richmond and threatening the Rebel rear. The Confederates would be forced to abandon Manassas Junction and fall back some 15 miles to the next defensible line, along the Rappahannock River. Washington could then breathe more easily.

With the flanking movement, McDowell hoped to force a Rebel retreat without a pitched battle, which could cripple his fledgling army. The success of his plan hinged partly on intimidating Beauregard's forces with superior numbers. "In proportion to the numbers used," he wrote, "will be the lives saved." But his strategy also depended on events farther west. If Joseph E. Johnston's army in the Shenandoah Valley managed to slip past the harassing Union forces of Major General Robert Patterson and fall on McDowell's right flank, the results might be catastrophic. McDowell admitted to Scott that he felt "very tender" about this possibility, but the general in chief assured him that his old friend Patterson would keep Johnston pinned down.

The projected date for launching the offensive, the 8th of July, proved unrealistic. In the midst of preparations, McDowell added a reserve division to his order of battle and the army swelled to 35,000 men, making it the largest force ever mustered in North America. (George Washington's combined Franco-American army at Yorktown numbered only 16,000, and General Scott had never led more than 13,000 men into battle.) It took another week of hectic prepa-ration before McDowell was ready to march.

At 2 p.m. on July 16, the Yankee army lurched off toward an enemy with forces of roughly equal size and inexperience.

At Manassas Junction, about 25 miles ahead of the Yankees, McDowell's former classmate (West Point class of 1838) and present rival waited anxiously for the Federal onslaught. General P.G.T. Beauregard had spent June and the early part of July suffering through the same delays and shortages that had plagued the Yankees. His plans had changed too, shifting back and forth between the attack and the defense. At last an edict from Richmond forbade him to take the offensive. President Davis and General Lee knew that the army was not strong enough, and feverishly they kept hurrying more regiments forward from all over the South. Meanwhile, Beauregard weighed his own readiness. He wrote that his soldiers "seem to have the most unbounded confidence in me. Oh, that I had the genius of a Napoleon!" Modest disclaimers never quite rang true coming from Beauregard.

As additional regiments came up from the Confederate capital, Beauregard fed them into his long battle line. Though he had built earthworks at Centreville, he came to realize that the village could be easily outflanked, and that the most logical line of defense was the south bank of Bull Run, which snaked between Centreville and Manassas Junction. Bull Run's five-foot-high banks were a formidable barrier. Only one bridge, a stone span on the Warrenton Turnpike, could support the wagon traffic of an army. But the stream could be forded in several places, so Beauregard had to spread his army thin to defend all the fords.

111

Seated among his aides, Union General in Chief Winfield Scott signs the order for General Irvin McDowell's advance against Confederate forces at Bull Run. Scott planned to accompany the army in a carriage, to be on hand in case his advice was needed during the battle, but his age and ill-health forced him to relinquish the idea.

The northernmost crossing was Sudley Ford, roughly two and a half miles upstream from the Stone Bridge. The roads leading to it from Centreville were circuitous and little known: Beauregard doubted that McDowell would try them, and he left them unguarded. The next crossing downstream was the Stone Bridge, which Beauregard discounted as a Yankee route on the grounds that it was too obvious, defending it only with a new half-brigade of South Carolina and Louisiana men under Colonel Nathan Evans.

At first glance, Evans was not a soldier who inspired confidence. An insubordinate, gruff, boastful South Carolinian, he was followed everywhere by an orderly who carried a gallon container of whiskey strapped to his back. Evans affectionately called the contraption his "barrelita," and he was quite fond of its contents. One of Evans' staff wrote home that the colonel "is at the same time about the best drinker, the most eloquent swearer (I should say voluble) and the most magnificent bragger I ever saw." But he was also a man who loved to fight.

Downstream from the bridge, the next three fords crossed Bull Run in dense woods, obviously unsuitable for an advancing army and guarded only lightly by the brigade of Colonel Philip St. George Cocke. It was farther south, on a crescent-shaped bend of Bull Run, that Beauregard expected all the action. There, two and a half miles from the Stone Bridge, lay Mitchell's Ford, an enticing prospect for an aggressor. Served by a good branch road off the Warrenton Turnpike, Mitchell's Ford was on the most direct route between Centreville and Manassas

Junction, the Federal objective. Between Mitchell's Ford and Manassas Junction lay two miles of level, open plain over which McDowell's troops could march unimpeded until they reached the Confederate works protecting the junction.

Beauregard was so certain that the Yankees would strike across Mitchell's Ford that he placed more than half his army in the area. Brigadier General Milledge L. Bonham's brigade guarded Mitchell's Ford, and Brigadier General James Longstreet's stood half a mile downstream at Blackburn's Ford, another good crossing. Units of Brigadier General David R. Jones's brigade blocked McLean's Ford, half a mile farther along. Colonel Jubal A. Early's brigade was posted in the rear of the three as a reserve, not far from the home of Wilmer McLean. And another mile and a half downstream, Brigadier General Richard S. Ewell and his brigade guarded Union Mills Ford and the nearby bridge of the Orange & Alexandria Railroad.

When General Beauregard finished positioning his troops, the Confederate line along Bull Run stretched for five miles from the Stone Bridge to Union Mills. No fewer than five of his army's seven brigades held the right half of the line.

But when he packed his troops southeast of the Stone Bridge, Beauregard had more in mind than positioning the defense according to McDowell's likely course of action. He planned to attack across the fords there, outflank the Federal army and cut it off from Washington. Though Richmond had forbidden an offensive campaign, Beauregard fully intended to steal the initiative from the Federals. Since his success in this venture depended on timely and accurate information, he ordered his signal officer, Captain E. Porter Alexander, to build four signal towers along Bull Run and at Manassas Junction. Schooled in the new wigwag system of flag signals, Alexander would be able to give his commander early warning of enemy movements by what he called "aerial reconnaissance" from the towers.

Beauregard had another, more valuable source of information: messages from Southern sympathizers and paid Confederate spies in Washington. Though Federal guards had been posted at the Potomac River bridges and instructed to let no one cross into Virginia without a pass, it was not difficult to get through the Union lines. Rose O'Neal Greenhow, *doyenne* of Washington society and a productive spy for the Confederacy, entrusted her messages to young Virginia ladies who were anxious to serve the South on such romantic missions. Yankee soldiers were unlikely to suspect them of carrying secrets, and the belles could easily charm their way through the lines with smiling protestations that they were just going for a ride.

The intelligence from Washington soon warned of critical developments. On July 10, a woman named Bettie Duval was shown into General Bonham's tent. She unpinned her long hair and withdrew from its folds a note from the widow Greenhow stating that McDowell's army would probably move on July 16. On that date she sent confirmation: "McDowell has been ordered to advance." Beauregard received the message at 8 p.m., just six hours after the Federal army started west. Immediately he called in his outposts and prepared to defend Bull Run.

The three columns of Federals were in no hurry in their march. The men trekked through a thinly populated region of low,

Encampments of the 23rd New York and the 2nd New Jersey Volunteer Infantry Regiments sprawl along the Virginia side of the Potomac River. Visible across the

river in Washington, D.C., are two partially completed landmarks: the Washington Monument *(left)* and the Capitol dome *(right of center)*.

rolling hills, with dense forests and culti-
vated fields interspersed with many creeks,
few bridges, and soft stream bottoms that
bogged wagons to the axles. The swatches
of tangled brush dispelled any possibility of
cross-country travel. McDowell had to stick
to the roads, most of which were dirt tracks
so narrow that they squeezed a column into
the shape of an earthworm and slowed its
pace to a crawl.

The soldiers dragged their feet, sang and
bragged, choked on dust, sweltered in the
heat and humidity. The enlisted men casual-
ly broke ranks to stop for drinks of water, or

to wash the caked grime from their faces, or
to forage for chickens—all in defiance of the
best efforts of their officers to maintain order. Even officers yielded to the yen for
plunder. On one occasion during the march,
a kilted officer of the 79th New York Highlanders went running after a pig. During the
chase he leaped a rail fence, presenting what
a comrade called "such an exhibition of his
anatomy as to call forth a roar of laughter."
He never wore the kilt again.

Of greater concern, high-ranking officers
displayed poor judgment. The commander
of the southernmost column, Brigadier Gen-

General Irvin McDowell (*center*),
preparing for the first Union offensive
in early July of 1861, stands with his
staff on the steps of his headquarters,
the former home of Robert E. Lee
in Arlington, Virginia. His adjutant,
Captain James B. Fry, is on
McDowell's right, with arms folded.

eral Samuel P. Heintzelman, a distinguished veteran of the Mexican War and the Indian campaigns, was paying no attention when his lead regiment slowed down at a creek to cross single file on a log bridge. Heintzelman allowed his column to be held up for hours while crossing that creek. Finally one of his brigade commanders, Colonel Oliver O. Howard, ignored the log and marched his men across—through water only knee-deep.

When night fell, the columns kept marching; it was 10 p.m. before most troops reached their objective and were allowed to bivouac. None had hiked more than six miles. Early the next day, July 17, the march resumed. The middle column, commanded by Brigadier General David Hunter, began trickling into Fairfax Court House around 10 o'clock. The Confederates had departed in such haste that meals were found simmering over campfires; the food was greedily devoured by the Yankee vanguard. Soon the northernmost column, commanded by Brigadier General Daniel Tyler, and the reserve column led by Colonel Dixon S. Miles arrived and made camp around the town.

To the south, Heintzelman's column lost time steadily to the jumbled terrain. Their objective—crossing Bull Run at Union Mills and skirting the Confederates' right flank—seemed to be receding in the distance. When Heintzelman encamped in the evening, he could see smoke rising from the Orange & Alexandria Railroad bridge, set afire by the retreating Rebels.

McDowell, at Fairfax Court House, was sorely disappointed by the march. He had expected to take the Confederate garrison at Fairfax by surprise early that morning, but delays had given the Rebels ample opportunity to withdraw. The commander was also worried about Heintzelman, whose position was a mystery to him. McDowell had to know whether Heintzelman had crossed Bull Run on his flanking march. He determined to find out that night.

But first, McDowell issued orders for the next day. Having learned from scouts that Centreville was being abandoned by the Rebels, he ordered Tyler to pass through the village at first light, with Hunter and Miles following. Tyler was then to march toward Bull Run, simulating a noisy assault. McDowell did not tell Tyler how far he should go in his demonstration attack, but he said emphatically, "Do *not* bring on an engagement." Tyler was to give the impression that the Union army was marching directly toward Manassas, thereby masking Heintzelman's flanking maneuver.

After a brisk ride through the darkness, McDowell found Heintzelman early on July 18. But then, in a quick tour of the countryside, he learned what good maps might well have told him—that the terrain was too difficult for crossing Bull Run at Union Mills Ford and getting around the Confederate right flank. Instead, he ordered Heintzelman to wheel his column and move toward Centreville. McDowell would have to rethink his strategy.

While McDowell was meeting with Heintzelman, events to his right were getting out of hand. General Tyler was vigorously exceeding his orders. He moved out at 7 a.m., with Colonel Israel Richardson's brigade as vanguard. Richardson, a combative West Pointer seasoned in the Mexican and Seminole Wars, passed through Centreville without incident. As expected, Beauregard had pulled all of his troops out during the night.

Since the day was still young, Tyler decided to advance and take a closer look at the Bull Run fords south of Centreville. He and Richardson rode two miles to a rise that overlooked Blackburn's Ford and, a few hundred yards west of it, Mitchell's Ford. Open fields ran down to Bull Run, but the stream was cloaked on both banks by trees and dense underbrush. Tyler spotted an enemy battery some distance behind the fords, and a few pickets here and there, but nothing else. He suspected that there might be more.

Tyler's orders were only to look, not to fight. Yet he thought he could see Manassas three miles off in the distance, and the idea of capturing the town tempted him. Would not the Rebels fall back before his attack, as they had done so far? He called up all of Richardson's brigade and began making preparations to probe across Bull Run. While awaiting the infantrymen's arrival, Tyler ordered two 20-pounders to open fire on the Confederate battery, and he sent forward two companies of the 1st Massachusetts as skirmishers to smoke out Confederates along the creek, forcing them to reveal their positions and strength.

The Massachusetts men, commanded by Colonel George D. Wells, soon discovered that a few houses and stands of trees on their side of the run concealed Rebel marksmen, and an hour of spirited skirmishing ensued as the Confederates staged a fighting withdrawal back across Bull Run. The closer the Yankees came to the stream, the hotter grew the Rebel resistance. When Colonel Wells brought his two companies out of the cover of a ravine and into the open directly above the stream, they were caught in a heavy cross fire that poured out of hidden positions up and down the tree-lined south bank. "We were in the thick of it full 15 minutes," Wells

wrote the next day, "the balls humming like a beehive. I am sure I shall see nothing so close hereafter."

As the balance of the Federal brigade reached the scene, Wells withdrew his companies, leaving several men killed. Doubts arose about the wisdom of continuing the engagement. Captain James B. Fry, McDowell's adjutant, rode up and advised Tyler to call a halt; the general's demonstration had uncovered the enemy's position and strength, and that was enough. But Tyler had the smell of powder in his nostrils. He had a full brigade on hand, and he wanted to attack. Ignoring Fry's arguments, the general ordered Richardson to move his brigade forward. They were about to discover that Beauregard had more than half of his army directly in front of them.

Richardson set up a line on the hillcrest half a mile north of the fords. He put a battery out in the open on the road and positioned the 2nd and 3rd Michigan and the 1st Massachusetts on the right of the guns, facing Mitchell's Ford, and the 12th New York on the left, poised above Blackburn's. The hilltop regiments were exposed and uncomfortably within range of the Confederate artillery and random shots from the concealed Rebel riflemen. "We made excellent marks for the enemy, who commenced firing at us," wrote one Michigan private. "The bullets whistled musically around us."

At this point, General Tyler abruptly decided that it was time to call off the attack. The increasing fire coming out of the wooded banks suggested that he was getting in over his head. His decision was correct, but its timing was lamentable. The general had gone forward with a squadron of Regular Army cavalry and Battery E, 3rd U.S. Artil-

A Major's Last Letter Home

Sullivan Ballou, a 32-year-old Providence lawyer and former Speaker of the Rhode Island House of Representatives, left a promising political career to enlist as a major in the 2nd Rhode Island Volunteers. From a camp near Washington, Ballou wrote a poignant letter *(right)* to his wife, Sarah, predicting his own death. At Bull Run a week later, he fell mortally wounded.

July 14, 1861
Camp Clark, Washington

My very dear Sarah:

The indications are very strong that we shall move in a few days—perhaps tomorrow. Lest I should not be able to write again, I feel impelled to write a few lines that may fall under your eye when I shall be no more. Our movements may be of a few days duration and full of pleasure—and it may be one of some conflict and death to me. "Not my will, but thine, O God be done." If it is necessary that I should fall on the battle field for my Country, I am ready.

I have no misgivings about, or lack of confidence in the cause in which I am engaged, and my courage does not halt or falter. I know how strongly American Civilization now leans on the triumph of the Government, and how great a debt we owe to those who went before us through the blood and sufferings of the Revolution. And I am willing—perfectly willing—to lay down all my joys in this life, to help maintain this Government, and to pay that debt.

But my dear wife, when I know that with my own joys, I lay down nearly all of your's, and replace them in this life with cares and sorrows, when after having eaten for long years the bitter fruits of orphanage myself, I must offer it as the only sustenance to my dear little children, is it weak or dishonorable, that while the banner of my forefathers floats calmly and fondly in the breeze, underneath my unbounded love for you, my darling wife and children should struggle in fierce, though useless contests with my love of Country.

I cannot describe to you my feelings on this calm Summer Sabbath night, when two-thousand men are sleeping around me, many of them enjoying perhaps the last sleep before that of death, while I am suspicious that death is creeping around me with his fatal dart, as I sit communing with God, my Country and thee. I have sought most closely and diligently and often in my heart for a wrong motive in thus hazarding the happiness of those I love, and I could find none. A pure love of my Country and of the principles I have so often advocated before the people—another name of Honor that I love more than I fear death, has called upon me and I have obeyed.

Sarah my love for you is deathless, it seems to bind me with mighty cables that nothing but Omnipotence could break; and yet my love of Country comes over me like a strong wind and burns me unresistably on with all these chains to the battle field.

The memories of the blissful moments I have spent with you come creeping over me, and I feel most gratified to God and to you that I have enjoyed them so long. And hard it is for me to give them up and burn to ashes the hopes of future years, when, God willing, we might still have lived and loved together, and seen our sons grown up to honorable manhood, around us. I have, I know, but few and small claims upon Divine Providence, but something whispers to me—perhaps it is the wafted prayer of my little Edgar, that I shall return to my loved ones unharmed. If I do not my dear Sarah, never forget how much I love you, and when my last breath escapes me on the battle field, it will whisper your name. Forgive my many faults, and the many pains I have caused you. How thoughtless and foolish I have often times been! How gladly would I wash out with my tears every little spot upon your happiness, and struggle with all the misfortunes of this world to shield you, and your children from harm. But I cannot. I must watch you from the Spirit-land and hover near you, while you buffit the storm, with your precious little freight, and wait with sad patience, till we meet to part no more.

But, O Sarah! if the dead can come back to this earth and flit unseen around those they loved, I shall always be near you; in the gladest days and in the darkest nights, advised to your happiest scenes and gloomiest hours, *always, always*, and if there be a soft breeze upon your cheek, it shall be my breath, as the cool air fans your throbbing temple, it shall be my spirit passing by. Sarah do not mourn me dead; think I am gone and wait for thee, for we shall meet again.

As for my little boys—they will grow up as I have done, and never know a father's love and care. Little Willie is too young to remember me long—and my blue eyed Edgar will keep my frolicks with him among the dim memories of childhood. Sarah I have unlimited confidence in your maternal care and your development of their characters, and feel that God will bless you in your holy work.

Tell my two Mothers I call God's blessing upon them. O! Sarah I wait for you there; come to me and lead thither my children.

Sullivan

lery, to take a close look himself, intending to use these two units to cover Richardson's advance. But now, having decided to withdraw, Tyler pulled them back just as Richardson sent forward the 12th New York. The New Yorkers would be left out on a limb.

"There were pine underbrush very thick, ahead of us," a New Yorker later recalled, "and as we marched into them about one or two rods, not thinking of danger quite so near, the bushes seemed to be alive with the Rebels." The trees and brush across the stream suddenly erupted with flame. "Their first volley was the most murderous to us," said a private. The Confederate fusillade forced them to the ground. They returned fire and rolled over on their backs to reload

their weapons and ram the charges home. After firing several rounds, the men found that the barrels of their guns were too hot to touch. The Yankees took whatever cover they could find, and for half an hour or more the firing along the run continued.

The Confederates were stiffening after a shaky beginning. The attack at first caught them off guard; they were lounging among the streamside shade trees when news of Tyler's advance came in from scouts. The men were still at their ease when the Federals reached the crest north of them and opened fire with their artillery. The first Yankee projectile made a sound "more like the neigh of an excited or frightened horse than anything I can compare it to," wrote Private

Centreville, Virginia, the northern gateway to the Bull Run battlefield, stands bleak and depopulated eight months after the clash. The strategic village, from which seven roads radiated, changed hands five times in the course of the War.

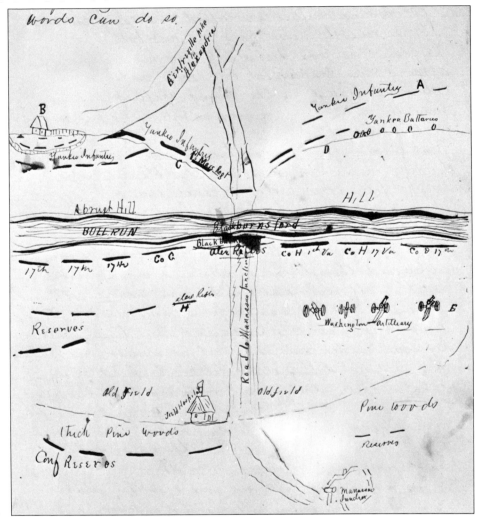

This crude map, drawn by Private Alexander Hunter of the 17th Virginia Infantry, depicts the positions of both sides in the skirmish at Blackburn's Ford on July 18, 1861. Though Hunter's outfit stopped Union troops from crossing Bull Run, he conceded that "if we had known more about military affairs, we could have seen at a glance our bad position."

William Morgan of the 11th Virginia, "a kind of 'whicker, whicker, whicker' sound as it swapped ends in the air."

As the skirmishing got heavier, the Confederate commander at Blackburn's Ford, General Longstreet, was forced to stand behind some of his men, sword drawn, to prevent them from breaking and running for the rear. But soon they were joined by reinforcements from Early's nearby brigade. Beauregard himself was there urging them on.

The Confederates at Blackburn's Ford were simply too powerful for the 12th New York. After half an hour the New Yorkers began to retreat, not as a disciplined unit, but singly and in wavering groups. Within minutes they were in rout and did not stop even when they reached the rest of Richardson's forces. Their flight from the field left the flank of the neighboring 1st Massachusetts completely exposed—"in the air."

Then Longstreet ordered his 1st and 17th Virginia to attack across the stream. The men of the 1st Massachusetts caught the full force of the onslaught and they, too, had to fall flat to escape the withering fire. The Michigan regiments on the far right of the Federal line were still facing Mitchell's Ford and playing the role of spectators. But before long the attacking Confederates made them targets, and soon the entire Yankee front was on the ground.

The fiery Colonel Richardson—his men called him "Fighting Dick"—wanted to rally the New Yorkers and send his whole brigade in at a charge. But by now Tyler had had quite enough, and he ordered the colonel to pull out of the fight. Reluctantly Richardson withdrew his battered brigade, and the tired Rebels returned to the south bank. The battle at Blackburn's Ford was over, though the artillery of the two sides continued to rumble for another hour or so.

As the battle ended, the scene in the rear of Tyler's command was bedlam. His brigades continued to arrive, only to see hundreds of panicked soldiers running in all directions. Colonel William T. Sherman rode up and reported "the always sickening confusion" one observed when approaching a fight from the rear.

McDowell himself arrived and berated Tyler for his breach of orders and the humiliating Federal performance. Only half of Richardson's 3,000 men had participated, against 2,500 of Longstreet's and portions of Early's 2,600-man brigade. Richardson had lost 19 killed, 38 wounded, and another 26 missing and probably captured. The Confederates had suffered slightly lower casualties—15 killed and 53 wounded—and they had enjoyed the sight of the fleeing Federals.

The Federals marched back toward Centreville, tired, angry, frustrated. "I know I felt mad and anxious to try it again," a Michigan private confided to his diary that night. Sherman was livid over the bungled battle, but not at all surprised. Two days before, on July 16, the army's unpreparedness had prompted him to write, "I still regard this as but the beginning of a long war." Blackburn's Ford did nothing to persuade him otherwise.

For the next two days, McDowell sat around Centreville and developed a new attack plan. He had been correct in discarding his original plan to flank Beauregard at Union Mills; the fight at Blackburn's Ford had proved that the enemy's center and right were too strong, and the ground too heavily wooded. McDowell now decided to circle the Confederates' left, masking the maneuver with a demonstration at the Stone Bridge and nearby fords. A reconnaissance report on July 19 informed McDowell that Sudley Ford, two and a half miles north of the Stone Bridge, seemed to be a suitable crossing for the flanking column. The general learned nothing, however, of the sinuous and confusing roads that led to Sudley Ford.

McDowell hoped to march on the 20th of July, but delays in the arrival of supplies forced him to postpone the advance until the next day. While the men sat in their camps

screwing up their courage, they watched and were watched by a throng of civilians from Washington who had followed the army to witness the grandest spectacle of their time—the thrashing of the Rebels. Several hundred people had arrived in buggies or on horseback, including senators, congressmen, and ladies with picnic baskets. Secretary of War Cameron was on hand. So was the prominent Washington photographer Mathew Brady, who would try unsuccessfully to capture the coming battle with his camera. Congressman John A. Logan of Illinois came to join the fight as an infantryman. Since his state had no unit on the field, he offered to fight in a Michigan regiment. He went into battle wearing top hat and tails.

Every few hours, the Federals heard train whistles blowing from the junction at Manassas. Most of the Yankees assumed the trains were bringing small numbers of unorganized troops from Richmond for Beauregard. Few chose to believe the rumors that those trains arriving on July 20 were bringing with them the first of General Johnston's brigades from the Shenandoah.

Johnston had been summoned by telegraph after the clash at Blackburn's Ford. Eluding the Federal army of General Patterson at Winchester, Johnston made an exhausting overland march to Piedmont Station on the Manassas Gap line and began shipping his four brigades east on July 19. The engines and cars were in poor condition and the roadbed was not much better, but by the afternoon of that day General Thomas J. Jackson and his Virginia brigade had arrived at Manassas Junction.

As soon as Jackson's men jumped from the cars, the train steamed back toward Piedmont Station to pick up the Georgia brigade

Briefly detraining during their hasty journey to Bull Run, troops of General Joseph E. Johnston are plied with refreshments by Confederate women at a station on the Manassas Gap Railroad. In two days, 9,000 soldiers traveled 50 miles by rail from the Shenandoah Valley to Manassas Junction en route to the battlefield.

commanded by Colonel Francis S. Bartow, a lawyer and politician from Savannah. The Georgians reached Manassas after dawn on July 20. Shortly after noon, Brigadier General Barnard E. Bee, a dignified South Carolinian who had served with gallantry in the Mexican War, arrived at the junction with his brigade, an amalgam of volunteers from several states. Another brigade, led by Brigadier General Edmund Kirby Smith, a former major in the Regular Army, would follow from the Valley. This massive reinforcement by railroad was progressing under the nose of the Federals.

Beauregard was also receiving fresh troops from other quarters. A small brigade led by Brigadier General Theophilus H. Holmes arrived from Aquia Creek on the lower Poto-mac. And Colonel Wade Hampton, a dynamic South Carolina planter and politician, arrived with his Hampton Legion, which he had raised, fed, clothed and armed at his own expense. The legion had its own infantry, artillery and cavalry companies, though the cavalry had not yet arrived when Hampton joined Beauregard.

General Johnston reached the junction on the afternoon of July 20. Because Johnston was the senior general, he automatically became the commander of the entire Confederate force, Beauregard's army as well as his own. But since he was unfamiliar with the terrain and the deployment of troops, Johnston left Beauregard in command. He immediately approved Beauregard's plan for an attack across the lower fords of Bull Run

123

at daybreak on the 21st of July to get behind McDowell's left flank and cut him off from Washington.

Beauregard's disposition of the new troops was, as before, distinctly unbalanced. He put Holmes's brigade at Union Mills to bolster Ewell, and sent Bee and Bartow to support Longstreet at Blackburn's Ford. Jackson and his Virginians were placed in reserve at Mitchell's Ford. None of the troops were sent to the left half of the line to protect the upper fords. So certain was Beauregard of McDowell's intentions that Sudley Ford remained unguarded.

To compound the danger, Beauregard proceeded to draft thoroughly confusing battle orders for his field commanders. Even though the largest organizational unit in his army was the brigade, Beauregard referred to divisions without saying which brigades constituted them, and he implied that certain divisions would combine to form two corps—although he did not actually use the word "corps." Moreover, he hinted that General Holmes would command one corps, but never told Holmes of this half-formed notion. It appeared that Beauregard intended to ignore the benefits of his massive reinforcements by attacking McDowell with just the brigades of Cocke and Bonham.

On the other side of Bull Run, McDowell called his own last council of war at 8 p.m. on July 20 at his Centreville headquarters. Spreading his inadequate map on the dirt floor of his tent, he made his assignments. Tyler, as if in punishment for Blackburn's Ford, was to be mostly a spectator, demonstrating at the Stone Bridge and the middle fords to hold the attention of the Rebels in his front. Once the battle was joined, he was expected to cross the creek. Miles would

First Unit Banners of the Confederacy

Early in the War, virtually every Confederate company boasted its own unique flag, created by local women and presented to the unit with great ceremony. Most of the banners were about six feet long and made of homespun cotton. In design, they commonly included elements of the Confederate Stars and Bars flag, and state symbols, such as a palmetto for South Carolina.

Before long, however, Confederate officers realized that it was dangerous for every outfit to fly its own flag; soldiers in battle depended for their very lives on quickly identifying nearby units. So the early flags were generally replaced by standard regimental battle flags, such as the one below. This banner has 13 stars, 11 for the Confederate states plus two for states claimed by the Confederacy: Kentucky and Missouri.

ARMY OF NORTHERN VIRGINIA BATTLE FLAG

MARION ARTILLERY, SOUTH CAROLINA MILITIA

8TH ARKANSAS INFANTRY REGIMENT

1ST LOUISIANA INFANTRY BATTALION

FLORIDA INDEPENDENT BLUES, 3RD FLORIDA INFANTRY REGIMENT

VIRGINIA BRIGADE FLAG

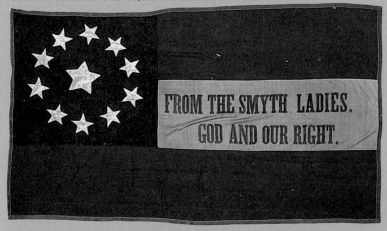

SMYTH DRAGOONS, 8TH VIRGINIA CAVALRY REGIMENT

General Beauregard doffs his cap to a regiment of boisterous Mississippi soldiers as they pass in ragged review, brandishing bowie knives. The high spirits of such units were due largely to Beauregard's style of leadership; he often dropped in on their camps to mix with the rank and file.

stay in reserve near Centreville. Hunter's and Heintzelman's divisions would march to Sudley Ford, cross, and then strike the enemy's left flank.

McDowell told his officers that he hoped to get behind the Confederates and drive on to the Manassas Gap line "before Johnston's men get there." Clearly—and, of course, correctly—McDowell had little confidence that Patterson was doing his job of holding Johnston in the Shenandoah.

General Tyler, smarting under criticism for Blackburn's Ford, asked McDowell just what army they would be fighting tomorrow: Beauregard's, or Beauregard's and Johnston's together? McDowell replied impatiently, "You know as well as I do."

Tyler would not let it pass. "General, we have got the whole of Joe Johnston's army in our front, and we must fight the two ar-

mies." McDowell had no choice but to continue with his plan. His army would march at 2 a.m. and attack at dawn.

What was left of the night passed quietly. McDowell stayed in his tent with a stomachache. Sherman wrote to his wife, "I know tomorrow and next day we shall have hard work." Colonel Howard, an intensely religious man who felt that Tyler's defeat had been punishment for the army's wicked ways, expressed the conviction that "the Lord will take care of us."

The men in the army tensed for the battle. Many could not sleep. Some gazed heavenward. "This is one of the most beautiful nights that the imagination can conceive," wrote a Yankee soldier. "The sky is perfectly clear, the moon is full and bright, and the air is as still as if it were not within a few hours to be disturbed by the roar of cannon and the shouts of contending men." Sitting around their campfires awaiting the order to march, the men watched the flames cast ghostly shadows into the fields and woods. They listened to the lowing of cattle in the meadows and the music from their regimental bands. Thousands of last letters were written home that night, expressing hopes for survival, acknowledging the possibility of death.

When the Yankees were awakened at 2 a.m., everything began to go wrong. It took another hour to get Tyler's lead brigade, commanded by Brigadier General Robert C. Schenck, ready to advance, and then its pace was snail-like. McDowell had committed a serious mistake. Tyler's brigade, which had the shortest distance to travel—straight down the Warrenton Turnpike to the Stone Bridge—should have been the last one to move out. Instead, Hunter and Heintzelman, who had farther to go in their flanking march to Sudley Ford, were severely de-

layed. Realizing his error after an hour on the march, General McDowell belatedly ordered Tyler's division off the road to let the others pass.

Everywhere, men stumbled and fell in the dark, bruising themselves and cursing aloud. A mile out of Centreville the vanguard came to Cub Run, a little stream spanned by a single rickety bridge. The crossing of the whole army was foolishly delayed for another half hour while a big 30-pounder cannon of Tyler's was coaxed over the fragile span. It was 5 a.m. before Schenck's advance brigade finally approached the Stone Bridge. And it was 6 a.m. before the 30-pounder fired three shots—resounding blasts that told the entire Federal army that Tyler was at last in place.

Hunter and Heintzelman should have arrived at Sudley Ford by then, and they should have been standing poised and ready to move down the south bank of Bull Run to strike Evans' troops at the Stone Bridge. But

William Weir's house near Manassas Junction served as General Beauregard's headquarters in the weeks before the Battle of Bull Run. After the battle, Jefferson Davis conferred with Beauregard in the house; a year later General Irvin McDowell took the house for his headquarters and was visited there by Abraham Lincoln.

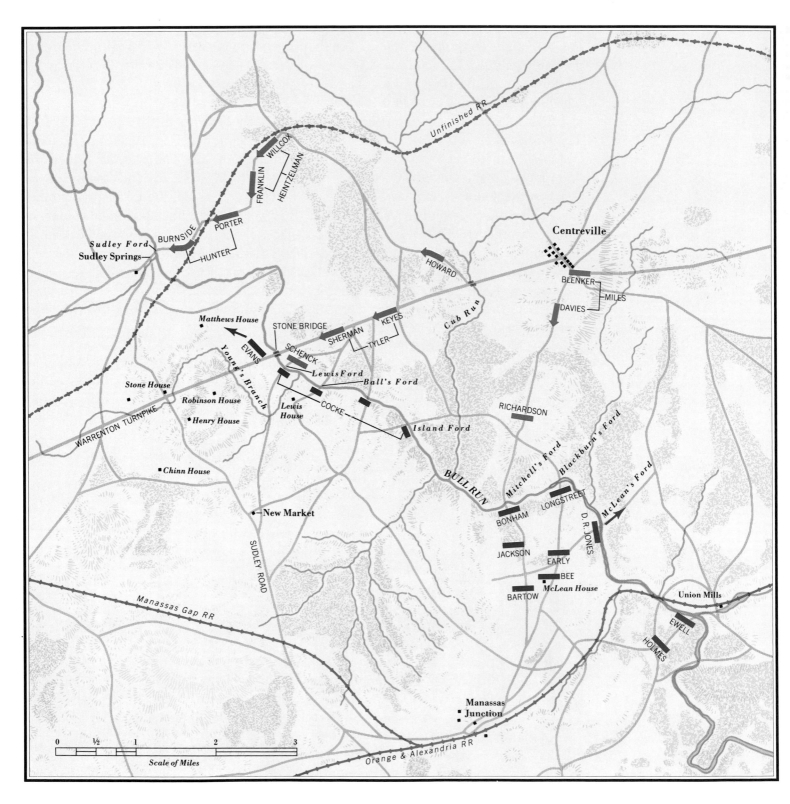

The battle at Bull Run began as the
Union brigades of Colonel Burnside
and Colonel Porter (*blue arrows,
upper left*) reached Sudley Ford at
9:30 a.m. on July 21 after a dawn
march from Centreville. Three
brigades under General Heintzelman
followed to bolster the Federal right
as other Union troops feinted toward
the Stone Bridge and Mitchell's Ford.
General Beauregard's Confederate
brigades (*red boxes*) were spread over
a six-mile front, with most on the
right. Only Colonel Evans' half-
brigade (*red arrow*) moved to counter
the threat to the Rebel left flank.

General Joseph E. Johnston, the
ranking Confederate officer at Bull
Run, jeopardized a longtime
friendship when he entrusted the
battlefield command to General
P.G.T. Beauregard. Though the two
men cooperated during the battle,
they later quarreled bitterly over who
deserved more credit for the victory.

Hunter's march had been further delayed
by puzzling forks in the road; a wrong turn
had added four miles to Hunter's route. At
9 a.m., his lead brigade reached the ford.

For all that, McDowell had gotten the
jump on his foe by the feint at the Stone
Bridge. Only Nathan Evans' troops stood
there to meet the enemy. Evans needed reinforcements, and fast. Yet Evans, more
than any other man, was to determine the
outcome of the battle.

As Tyler appeared in his front, Evans
wisely kept his tiny command hidden in the
woods behind a rise south of the bridge. He
had only a squadron of cavalry, two fieldpieces, his 4th South Carolina Regiment
and Major Roberdeau Wheat's 1st Louisiana
Special Battalion, styled "Wheat's Tigers,"
a unit notable for its red shirts and belligerence. Wheat was a man much like Evans in

his appetite for fighting; he was a veteran of
the Mexican War and had been a filibuster
in Central America and a warrior for Giu-
seppe Garibaldi during the war for Italian
unification. Standing six feet four inches tall
and weighing nearly 300 pounds, Wheat was
an imposing figure on the battlefield—to
friend and foe alike.

Evans moved with speed and confidence.
He sent two companies of the 4th South
Carolina down toward the bridge to act as
skirmishers, but he refused to show the balance of his command. For nearly an hour his
skirmishers alone returned fire, while the
rest of his line, including the cannon, remained silent. When at last Evans opened
with his fieldpieces, he still kept most of his
infantry concealed. He was surprised at first
that Tyler did not attempt to cross the
bridge; he did not guess that Tyler was there
only to hold his attention. But by 7:30, Evans had realized that "it was not the intention
of the enemy to attack me in my present position." He therefore was free to use the bulk
of his command to meet another threat.

Evans had stationed a few pickets to his
left and a couple of cavalrymen off to the
north around Sudley Ford. One of the sen-
tries warned Evans that Yankees had been
sighted marching toward Sudley Ford. At
the same time Captain Alexander, perched
on an observation tower and scanning the
horizon with his field glasses, spotted the sun
glinting off Hunter's bayonets and bronze
cannon north of the Stone Bridge. Quickly
Alexander wigwagged to a second tower,
which was on the hill just behind Evans.
"Look out on your left," warned Alexander,
"you are turned."

In view of the overwhelming odds against
him, Colonel Evans could have withdrawn

Opening the battle at Bull Run, the main Union column of 18,000 men swings into action at 9:30 a.m. on July 21, 1861. An artist sketches the scene for a Northern newspaper, while an officious civilian (right) questions a staff officer.

without apology. Instead, he decided to attack. He left four companies of the South Carolinians to face Tyler's troops at the bridge, then led the rest of his command north over farm tracks to the crest of Matthews Hill, barely a mile south of Sudley Ford. Here Evans deployed his men under cover of woods, with a good view of the cleared fields that Hunter would have to cross. The 4th South Carolina went into line on the left, with one fieldpiece, while Wheat's Tigers and the other gun held the right. Shortly after 9 a.m. Evans was ready, and none too soon. At 9:15 the men saw the vanguard of Hunter's column march out of the trees that shaded Sudley Ford.

In the Federal vanguard were two Rhode Island regiments from the brigade of Colonel Ambrose E. Burnside. Hunter himself was leading them as they started up Matthews Hill. Evans' first volley stopped them in

their tracks and pinned them down on the slope. Hunter was seriously wounded in the neck and left cheek while attempting to rally the men and lead them forward in a bayonet assault. Then Colonel John Slocum of the 2nd Rhode Island took a mortal wound as he climbed a fence to wave his men on. As the injured officers were carried from the field, Hunter told Burnside, "I leave the matter in your hands."

Burnside speedily brought the rest of his brigade into the battle line, only to have his fresh regiments mauled. Intense Rebel fire killed Burnside's horse under him and convinced the colonel that Evans must have six regiments of infantry and two batteries of artillery on Matthews Hill. To Burnside's right, Colonel Andrew Porter began to bring his regiments into line, meaning the Federals now had more than a brigade facing only a regiment and a battalion of Confederates.

The Yankees were adjusting their line, shifting troops and artillery, when Porter and Burnside saw the Rebels suddenly swarm down the slope toward them.

Roberdeau Wheat must have seemed insane to some of his troops. They were overwhelmingly outnumbered, yet their commander ordered a charge with only part of his flimsy line. And they were insane enough to follow his order. Wheat and his 500-odd Louisiana Tigers raced down the slope and plunged into the off-guard Yankee regi-

ments. The Rebels came on screaming, some waving bowie knives over their heads.

Although the Tigers could not hope to dislodge Porter and Burnside, their wild charge threw the Federals into confusion—and that was all Evans needed. Confusion would buy time for Beauregard to get reinforcements to Matthews Hill. But it was time bought at the cost of 48 casualties among the Louisianians.

Major Wheat was hit hard. A bullet struck him just under one armpit, plowed through his chest and came out the other side. His

Sudley Ford, where Yankee troops waded across Bull Run to attack the Confederate left, flows quietly again eight months later, deserted except for a farm boy perched atop the stone springhouse. Sudley Church, at the top of the ridge, was a major landmark during the fighting; the Federals used it as a field hospital.

soldiers wrapped him in the regimental flag and carried him to the rear, where surgeons told him he had suffered a mortal wound. "I don't feel like dying yet," Wheat protested. The doctors said that in all their experience no one had ever recovered from such a wound. "Well, then," said Wheat, "I will put my case upon record." And he did, surviving the wound to fight again.

After the Tigers were beaten back, Evans realized that his sally had run its course. He could see the Yankee line spreading out farther on his left flank, and he knew that he could not hold his position much longer. More signal messages arrived, warning that Heintzelman's column was crossing at Sudley Ford. It was time to pull back before being overwhelmed. But Evans had performed a remarkable feat, holding a vastly superior force at bay just long enough for his own support to arrive.

General Bee's brigade, the first of the Confederate reinforcements, came rushing up to the army's threatened left, followed closely by the brigade of Colonel Bartow. Bee had been angry that morning when Beauregard ordered him off toward the Stone Bridge; he thought he would find only a skirmish and would miss the real battle, which everyone expected at Mitchell's Ford. But as Bee and his artillery commander, Captain John D. Imboden, rode over the crest of Henry House Hill, across the turnpike and Young's Branch to Matthews Hill, Bee was relieved to see that the main fight was looming here after all. He told Imboden, "Here is the battlefield, and we are in for it!"

Bee's and Bartow's men had marched nearly six miles that morning in broiling heat with little water, and they arrived on the battlefield, as one said, "breathless, footsore

Confederate Colonel Nathan Evans, called "Shanks" because of his skinny bowlegs, detected the Union flank attack at Sudley Ford and rushed to meet it, even though his brigade was greatly outnumbered. Evans' initiative held back the Yankees for more than an hour and was praised by General McDowell's adjutant as "one of the best pieces of soldiership on either side."

and exhausted, but eager for the fray." There was no time to rest or to slake their thirst. Bee led his men—the 4th Alabama and the 2nd and 11th Mississippi—to the right of Evans' line and moved them forward to within 100 yards of the Yankees. Bartow's men, the 7th and 8th Georgia, immediately went into line on Bee's right. The brigades fired a volley, lay down on the slope to reload, and jumped back up to fire again.

Bee and Bartow, like Evans before them, were merely buying time, waiting for reinforcements. But their chances, too, appeared poor. Though Imboden was wheeling his battery into action on Henry House Hill, Yankee troops kept pouring into line, extending it beyond the Rebels' left. If the Federals attacked with their entire line, nothing could stop them.

The whole Southern contingent on the hill now totaled perhaps 5,500—still only a third of the enemy's assault force. But the Con-

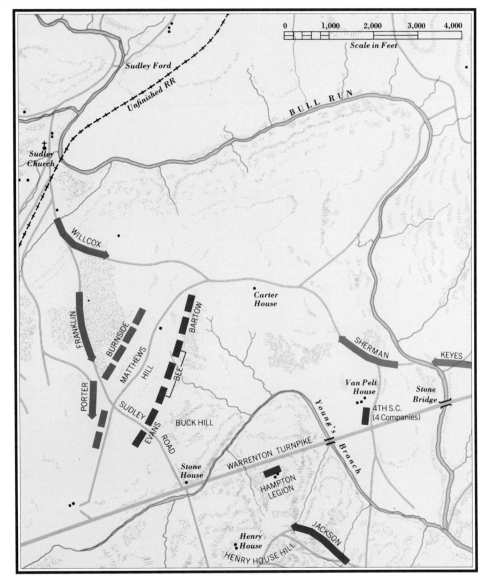

At 9:45 a.m., Colonel Evans' brigade confronted the vanguard of two Union divisions on Matthews Hill. Evans was reinforced by General Bee's brigade and Colonel Bartow's brigade. The Confederates managed to stall McDowell's offensive for nearly two hours, but finally they were flanked and routed by the brigades of Colonels Porter, Sherman and Keyes (*blue arrows*).

federate officers decided to attack again, giving more reinforcements time to join them. While they awaited the word to go forward, some thirsty, hungry Georgians began throwing rocks to knock apples out of a nearby tree. A few men even started to climb the tree, but Yankee cannon drove them down with a shell or two in their direction. "The boys dropped from the apple tree like shot bears," said a Georgian. Other soldiers spent

the time thinking somber thoughts. "I felt that I was in the presence of death," wrote one of Bartow's men. "My first thought was, 'This is unfair; somebody is to blame for getting us all killed. I didn't come out here to fight this way; I wish the earth would crack open and let me drop in.' "

At about 10:30 a.m., the whole Confederate line charged toward Burnside's and Porter's brigades. They caught heavy fire. Bartow's Georgians on the right flank bore the brunt of it, since they had no woods for cover. "The balls just poured on us, struck our muskets and hats and bodies," a soldier later wrote home. "This bold and fearful movement was made through a perfect storm."

The 8th Georgia finally reached a thicket within easy musket range of a Federal battery. They rained fire on the Yankee gunners and their infantry supports. The Federals returned their fire. "It was a whirlwind of bullets," recalled a survivor. "Our men fell constantly. The deadly missiles rained like hail among the boughs and trees." In one company of the 8th, five men were killed, 25 wounded, five more lost or captured. Bartow's horse was killed, the regimental adjutant was killed, and Lieutenant Colonel W. M. Gardner fell wounded. The Georgia men later named that grove "the place of slaughter."

While the Georgians were held up at the grove, Bee's brigade on their left pushed up a bald slope leading to Burnside's position. "Our brave men fell in great numbers," wrote Captain Thomas Goldsby of the 4th Alabama, "but they died as the brave love to die—with faces to the foe, fighting in the holy cause of liberty." That was how he preferred to remember it. They also died in the dirt, painfully, mixing their blood with the

red clay of Virginia. One company lost 30 men. Lieutenant Colonel J. B. Jones was mortally wounded, his leg shattered, and every other field officer of the 4th Alabama was killed or injured. When one of Bartow's aides rode across the rear of the Alabamians, his horse was struck and knocked down by eight bullets, and before he could pick himself up from the ground, five more bullets slammed into the dead animal. Now thousands of Federals were firing steadily and the air was alive with lead.

General Bee grew desperate. Neither Bartow's Georgians on his right nor Evans' weary men on his left had been able to keep up with his brigade. So both of Bee's flanks were exposed to enemy fire, and the Yankees were preparing to counterattack. Matthews Hill had at last become untenable. There was nothing to do but retire or be overwhelmed. Bartow and Evans were already pulling their remnants back over Matthews Hill to Young's Branch.

Now Bee's men withdrew under heavy fire, and again they suffered fearful casualties. Just as they were hastening down the

Colonel Ambrose Burnside, astride a rearing horse (*center*), urges his Rhode Island men up Matthews Hill. But Burnside's troops, shattered by withering Confederate fire, retreated and took no further part in the fight.

south slope of Matthews Hill, they saw a gray-clad regiment off toward the Stone Bridge. Bee's men thought the outfit must be reinforcements. An officer from the 4th Alabama made a signal of recognition and thought he saw it returned. The Alabamians moved to re-form their unit beside the new outfit. But when the Alabama regiment unfurled its Confederate colors, the other unit, said one of Bee's men, "opened a murderous fire upon our ranks." The newcomer was, in fact, Colonel William T. Sherman's 2nd Wisconsin, the gray-uniformed vanguard of a grave new threat to the Confederates.

Sherman's troops were part of Tyler's division, which had been sitting behind the Stone Bridge and doing nothing for several hours that morning. At 11 a.m., when Hunter's and Heintzelman's divisions resumed their advance, Tyler received McDowell's orders to attack across the Stone Bridge at once. Yet the memory of Blackburn's Ford loomed large in Tyler's mind, and he waited and worried for a time. Finally he ordered Colonel Sherman to take his 3,400-man brigade across Bull Run.

Sherman crossed the stream several hundred yards north of the Stone Bridge at a shallows that he had reconnoitered that morning. The Yankees met almost no resistance from the four companies of South Carolinians left there by Evans. Within a few minutes, Sherman and his men came out of the woods several hundred yards north of the Warrenton Turnpike and headed directly for the Rebels' exposed flank. They were soon followed by the brigade of Colonel Erasmus D. Keyes.

When the Confederate troops falling back across Young's Branch realized that they were being overwhelmed on the flank as well as at the front, their withdrawal dissolved into a rout. Out of control, soldiers abandoned the line and raced across the Warrenton Turnpike and up the north slope of Henry House Hill. In spite of their magnificent performance that morning, Bee, Bartow and Evans were about to be engulfed by a tide of Yankees.

As the Rebels fled, Sherman joined Burnside and Porter near the Matthews house on the newly won hill. Heintzelman and McDowell were nearby, and they all watched as the Confederates fell back in what appeared to be a full-scale retreat. The commanding general immediately ordered Sherman's brigade to join in the pursuit, then McDowell himself mounted and rode along his advancing battle lines. A day that had begun so badly now seemed to be going perfectly. Two of his divisions had crossed Bull Run and a third was starting to cross. Despite the heavy casualties suffered by the forces under Burnside and Porter, McDowell's army was now rolling up the enemy. Once he reached the Warrenton Turnpike, just on the other side of Young's Branch, McDowell had only to push three miles down the road to reach the tracks of the Manassas Gap Railroad. There he would be able to cut off reinforcements from the Shenandoah Valley while advancing unimpeded to Manassas Junction and down the Orange & Alexandria Railroad toward Richmond.

Flushed with success after all the weeks of frustration, General McDowell rode jubilantly along his lines, standing in his stirrups and shouting to the advancing ranks, "Victory! Victory! The day is ours!" But his elation was premature.

Verdict on Henry House Hill

"The words, gestures, and threats of our officers were thrown away upon men who had lost all presence of mind and only longed for absence of body."

COLONEL ANDREW PORTER, U.S.A.

It was not a good morning for General Beauregard. He spent most of it at the McLean farm, his headquarters near Mitchell's Ford, in deepening perplexity and alarm. He heard only a little firing on his right, where five of his brigades were supposed to be crossing Bull Run to attack the Federal camps around Centreville. And not much was happening in front of him at Mitchell's Ford, where he expected the main enemy blow to fall. Instead, sounds of battle grew steadily in the northwest—his lightly defended left flank.

Nothing was going as Beauregard had planned, and for some time he was so paralyzed by confusion that he made no countermove. By 9:30 a.m. he had sent the brigades of Barnard Bee, Francis Bartow and Thomas Jackson to reinforce his threatened left. Then he again lapsed into inaction. Later he roused himself and framed orders calling the brigades of Richard Ewell, David Jones, Theophilus Holmes and James Longstreet back to the south bank of Bull Run.

As the morning slipped by, General Johnston listened intently to the sounds of battle and waited with growing anxiety for Beauregard to act. It seemed more and more obvious that Beauregard's orders had immobilized his army's right flank. Much more alarming was the situation on the left flank. Although Johnston had given his subordinate the battlefield command, Beauregard's evident inability to take control of the battle off to the left finally impelled Johnston to act. Shortly before noon, Johnston told Beauregard flatly that the left must be heavily reinforced. "The battle is there," he said. "I am going."

Johnston's decision apparently came as a great relief to Beauregard, lifting from his shoulders the ultimate responsibility for the battle and permitting him to think more clearly. "My heart for a moment failed me," he later admitted in his customary melodramatic manner. "I felt as though all was lost. I wished I had fallen in the battle of the 18th; but I soon rallied, and I then solemnly pledged my life that I would that day conquer or die!"

Beauregard ordered Holmes, Jubal Early and Milledge Bonham to start moving their commands toward the fighting on the left. He then decided to send Jones, Longstreet and Ewell back across Bull Run, thinking that perhaps the Centreville attack could be restored to the program. It was a frustrating day for the brigades that Beauregard kept moving back and forth across Bull Run; the soldiers never quite managed to dry their socks. But Beauregard had sent substantial reinforcements to his threatened left flank. His confidence rising, he rode off after Johnston toward the northwest to watch events unfold.

The battle was a desperate one for the three brigades that had been trying to hold off two Federal divisions for nearly two hours. By noon the Confederates had fallen back from Matthews Hill, across the Warrenton

This handsome uniform, worn on full-dress occasions by the 79th New York Highlanders, includes a kilt and blue jacket modeled after the dress of the British Army's Scottish troops. Before marching off to Bull Run, most of the Highlanders exchanged their kilts for either blue Army pants or trim tartan trousers called trews.

Turnpike and through the shallow waters of Young's Branch, and they had finally come to the crest of the hill where stood the Henry family's farmhouse.

The first reinforcements to reach these battered Confederates were the 600 South Carolinians of the Hampton Legion, fresh off a train from Richmond. Colonel Hampton had reported to General Bee just before the Confederate retreat began, and he had been ordered to act as a reserve, placing his men in a defensive position on Henry House Hill. But Hampton was interested in glory, not defense. He formed up his men in front of a white frame house owned by a freed slave named James Robinson, then marched them down the slope to the Warrenton Turnpike—just as the Confederate line broke. The retreating troops came rushing back toward Hampton's Legionnaires, then fled past them and up the hill.

Suddenly the Hampton Legion was all alone and in the forefront of the battle; for a while it was the only Confederate command still fighting. The South Carolinians were hard hit by Federal fire, their ranks torn by exploding shells from the crack Union batteries of Captains James B. Ricketts and Charles Griffin. A single shell tore off the foot of a lieutenant and killed three soldiers. Hampton's lieutenant colonel was killed and his own horse was shot from under him.

Realizing that his legion could no longer stand alone, Hampton withdrew to the cover of a wooded depression behind the Robinson house, 700 yards northeast of the Henry house. Now it seemed that nothing stood in the way of the Yankee advance.

But the Federal forces did not immediately pursue the retreating Confederates; General McDowell first found it necessary to re-

form his line along the Warrenton Turnpike at the foot of Henry House Hill. The dogged Rebel defense of Matthews Hill had taken a heavy toll, chewing up the advance units of the Union right wing. McDowell's commanders, particularly Andrew Porter and Ambrose Burnside, had squandered their forces during the morning, sending in attacks by single regiments rather than slamming ahead with entire brigades to overwhelm the outnumbered enemy defenders. Burnside had so depleted his brigade in piecemeal attacks that his only remaining effective force was a single regiment, the 2nd New Hampshire. General Heintzelman had already seen three regiments of the 11 in his division disorganized by enemy fire.

Despite his heavy losses of troops, McDowell retained a strong edge in available manpower. In re-forming his line, he placed the newly arrived brigade of Erasmus Keyes on his left, placed William Sherman's fresh brigade in the middle, and put Porter's battleworn units on the far right along with Orlando Willcox's and William Franklin's brigades. Burnside's decimated brigade was to be held in reserve. General Schenck's brigade, backed up by artillery, held the north end of the Stone Bridge. McDowell also deployed 24 pieces of artillery, including the 12 guns of the batteries commanded by Ricketts and Griffin. In all, he had some 11,000 infantrymen ready to advance once more by 2 p.m. A vigorous thrust up Henry House Hill would gain the smashing victory that McDowell had prematurely claimed.

Meanwhile, the Confederate left had been reinforced by General Jackson's five regiments of Virginia infantry. Jackson and his men had been awake since before dawn, preparing to support Longstreet in Beauregard's projected attack on Centreville. Anticipating a confused fight in tangled country and fearing bloody mistakes because some Union units wore gray uniforms while his own 33rd Virginia wore blue, Jackson instructed his men to identify themselves by tying strips of white cloth around their arms or hats. Further to identify themselves to one another, his men were to strike their left breasts with their right hands and shout, "Our homes!" Some soldiers found this routine a bit theatrical: "We presented the appearance of so many lunatics," one of them complained, adding, "They failed to tell us that while we were going through this Masonic performance, we thus gave the other fellow an opportunity to blow our brains out, if we had any."

When the fight on the left started, Jackson did not wait for orders but marched northward toward the sound of the guns. Sending word ahead to Bee that he was coming, he pushed his men some four miles from their bivouac near Mitchell's Ford to the reverse slope of Henry House Hill, arriving there shortly before noon.

Jackson did not rush into the fight, which was then raging around Young's Branch. Instead, he ordered his men to form a line just behind the crest of Henry House Hill. Exactly why Jackson stopped here remains a mystery. He may have decided that this was the best place to make a stand, which it arguably was (another who thought so was Captain Imboden, who moved his battery of artillery here after it had been driven from the crest of the hill by accurate Union fire). Further, Jackson was a stickler for orders. Having come to the battle line on his own initiative, he may have hesitated to do anything more without hearing from his superiors.

Confederate Colonel Francis S. Bartow, a Savannah lawyer before the War, made up for his lack of military experience with sheer hard work. "I sleep about five hours in the 24," he wrote his mother a month before the Bull Run battle, "and very seldom take off my clothes or even my shoes. My toilet is made in the morning by putting on my hat."

In any case, some of Jackson's Virginians were puzzled by their eccentric commander's decision to take a defensive position. "The firing in our front was terrific," a soldier recalled, "and why we did not render immediate and timely assistance to Bee I could never learn." Bee's retreating line did receive some support from the Confederate artillery commanded by Colonel William N. Pendleton. Elements of four batteries totaling 13 guns were now on the hill. Pendleton, an Episcopal minister, shouted the order, "Fire, boys! And may God have mercy on their guilty souls!" But Pendleton's efforts were not enough to stop the retreat, and the Confederate infantrymen were soon scrambling over the crest of Henry House Hill.

Bee rode up to Jackson and shouted, "General, they are beating us back!"

"Sir," said Jackson calmly, "we'll give them the bayonet."

Reassured, General Bee galloped back to his shattered force. Amid all the confusion, he recognized no one. "What regiment is this?" he demanded.

"Why, General, don't you know your own troops?" asked a soldier. "This is all that is left of the 4th Alabama."

Bee asked the battle-weary men to make

another effort. According to Captain Thomas Goldsby, he put the question thus: "Will you follow me back to where the firing is going on?" And his men answered with a cheer, "To the death!" It is more likely that Bee, known as a virtuoso swearer, said something more pithy to his men, and that their cheer may also have been less heroic and more flavorful.

Bee said something more before leading his men back into the fight. Several of those present recalled that their general pointed toward the nearby Virginia brigade and exclaimed that Jackson was standing there "like a stone wall." One of several latter-day accounts said that Bee added, "Let us determine to die here, and we will conquer."

Exactly what Bee said or meant is not

Brigadier General Barnard E. Bee, who rallied the collapsing Confederate left flank at Bull Run, showed early in his career that he had no patience with pettifogging regulations and no fear of disciplinarians. While attending the Military Academy at West Point, Bee accrued a large number of demerits, many for chewing tobacco on duty.

clear. In after days, Confederates would claim it was a tribute to the way Jackson and his men had stood under enemy fire. The trouble was that when Bee uttered his remark, Jackson's brigade was still lying low, not yet exposed to Federal bullets. Major Thomas Rhett of Jackson's staff later claimed that Bee had told him he was furious when Jackson had lodged on the hill "like a stone wall" instead of coming to his assistance. Whatever he meant, General Bee had given Jackson his nickname, Stonewall.

Bee quickly led the 4th Alabama forward over the crest of Henry House Hill and down the northern slope in an attempt to turn back the Federals. It was a gallant but hopeless effort. The Union artillery under Griffin and Ricketts battered the Alabamians so brutally that the men broke and ran once more, heading back over the crest of the hill. Bee was seen riding bravely through it all, trying to hold his command together in the face of panic. Later on, one of Jackson's Virginians saw the general turn his horse toward the enemy, as if deliberately riding to his death. Perhaps he did. Eventually, in front of the remnants of his brigade, Bee was shot off his horse, mortally wounded. His dying utterances, some said, were bitter recriminations against Jackson for not aiding him.

General Johnston and General Beauregard arrived at the front about the time Bee was vainly trying to patch together a new defensive line. The commanders found Jackson and his Virginians still in place behind the crest of Henry House Hill, with the Hampton Legion far to the right near the Robinson house. Behind this sketchy line they encountered bits and pieces left from the morning's bloody work. Some of Evans' and Bartow's troops had re-formed and were

now making their way back toward the front.

Johnston rode over to the shattered remnants of the 4th Alabama. The exhausted men were standing in line 300 yards to the rear. Johnston found the color sergeant and, with the sergeant carrying the regimental banner, led the 4th Alabama back to form on Jackson's right. Johnston also encountered the indomitable Nathan Evans, almost alone now but ready for more fight. Evans led his few surviving men into line on the right of the Alabamians while Bartow worked gallantly at re-forming his Georgia regiments. When Bartow reported to Beauregard, the general directed him to anchor the Georgians to Jackson's left.

With this patchwork of survivors and Jackson's brigade, the Confederate leaders had salvaged a defense out of what had seemed to be certain disaster just an hour before. The Confederates' line stabilized. Now, with the brigades of Early and Bonham on their way to the field, followed by Colonel Jeb Stuart's 1st Virginia Cavalry, Beauregard and Johnston paused to consider how to conduct the battle. It was decided that Johnston would take up a position in the rear and funnel reinforcements to Henry House Hill as they appeared. Beauregard, meanwhile, would continue to exercise tactical command of the battle, plugging new troops into the line as they arrived. Johnston

Confederate General Joseph E. Johnston (*foreground*), arriving at his threatened left flank to reorganize the sagging defense, rallies a Georgia regiment. Colonel Bartow, waving a flag at rear, gallops through enemy fire to regroup his shattered forces.

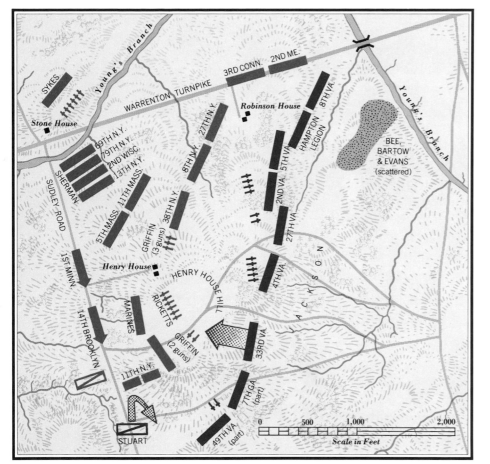

left, well concealed in a patch of woods.

By 2 p.m. the Confederates had perhaps 6,500 men and Pendleton's 13 cannon on the hill. But they still faced a foe that greatly outnumbered them, and Beauregard knew it. Now fully in command of the situation, Beauregard rode along his line, exhorting the men to stand fast, telling them that they need hold only a little longer until more reinforcements arrived. His horse was shot from under him, but he calmly picked himself up, found another mount and continued to oversee the defense.

The lull in the battle as the two forces reorganized soon came to an end. Jackson saw two Yankee batteries—Ricketts' and Griffin's—lumber down Buck Hill to the Warrenton Turnpike and start up the slope of Henry House Hill, obviously intent upon softening up the Confederate line before an infantry attack. Quickly Jackson sent news of the threat to Beauregard, then passed word among his Virginians that they were to stand ready on the ground back from the crest. But when the Yankees came up the slope, and "when their heads are seen above the hill, let the whole line rise, move forward with a shout, and trust to the bayonet." To his aides, Stonewall confided: "I am tired of this long-range work."

So was McDowell. The time he had taken reorganizing his line had surely given the Confederates the breathing space they needed to set up a new defense. It was high time to finish off the Rebels—pound them with close-range artillery fire and then put them to flight with a final bayonet charge. To his chief of artillery, Major William F. Barry, McDowell gave the order for Griffin and Ricketts to move their batteries forward.

Barry conveyed the order to Griffin, who

The turning point of the Bull Run battle was reached at about 2:30 p.m. The 33rd Virginia captured the exposed batteries of Captains Ricketts and Griffin near the crest of Henry House Hill, routing the units supporting the batteries—the 11th New York Fire Zouaves and a battalion of U.S. Marines. Federal reinforcements, led by the 14th Brooklyn, reached the scene too late to save the all-important artillery.

then rode to "Portici," the home of the Francis Lewis family, a mile south of the battle line on Henry House Hill.

Even as Johnston was establishing his new headquarters at Portici, fresh regiments reached Beauregard. Three companies from the 49th Virginia, commanded by elderly ex-governor William Smith, plus a scattering of surviving companies from other commands went into line on the extreme left; another Virginia regiment soon followed. Beauregard's idea was to extend the left of his battle line, guarding that flank against the ever-lengthening Yankee line opposite. When Jeb Stuart and his cavalry came up, Beauregard positioned them on the extreme

instantly protested. He would be advancing five guns—one had been disabled—without infantry support, making them easy prey for a Confederate counterattack. Barry assured him that the Union infantry would advance right behind him. The regiment would be the colorful 11th New York Fire Zouaves. Griffin, a Regular Army officer, confessed his fear that the Zouaves, green volunteers entering their first battle, would not stand firm under enemy fire. "Yes, they will," said Barry. "At any rate, it is General McDowell's order to go there." Griffin obeyed, but tossed a last warning over his shoulder: "I will go, but mark my words, they will not support us."

Griffin led the way, with Ricketts right behind him. They galloped their guns up the slope of Henry House Hill to within 300 yards of the Confederate line. If the Federal infantry did not support them quickly, they would make handsome targets for enemy marksmen and a ripe prize for capture if the Rebels advanced. Indeed, the Confederate fire began just as Ricketts brought his guns into battery—in line several yards apart, with the ammunition caissons and limbers several yards to the rear.

Bullets at once started bringing down his gunners and horses. Ricketts concluded that the shots came from the Henry house. Confederate marksmen were posted around the

Artillery Captain Charles Griffin, who was promoted to brevet major for his heroics at Bull Run, was much admired by his men for protecting their rights and promoting their welfare. Griffin was so outspoken in their defense that on at least one occasion his superiors almost arrested him for insubordination.

In a desperate charge to retake the captured Federal batteries of Griffin and his fellow artillerist, Captain James B. Ricketts, remnants of the New York Fire Zouaves (foreground), the Brooklyn Chasseurs and other units move up Henry House Hill. The wounded Ricketts was captured but later paroled; like Griffin, he became a Union general.

house and perhaps inside. The owner of the house, an elderly, invalid widow, Judith Henry, had been confined inside since the battle began swirling through her fields. She lay in an upstairs bedroom, waiting fearfully with her son, her daughter and a servant.

Ricketts quickly turned his guns and began slamming shells into the house. One shell tore through the wall of the widow's bedroom. A large fragment struck her bed, tearing away one of the old woman's feet and inflicting other wounds. She died before nightfall. Her son John lay on the ground outside, under the fire of both armies, crying out in anguish, "They've killed my mother!"

While Griffin and Ricketts followed McDowell's orders, Major Barry went looking for the Fire Zouaves to send them forward to support the batteries. He rounded up the 11th New York, the 14th Brooklyn Chasseurs and a battalion of U.S. Marines and led them across Young's Branch, then up the forward slope of Henry House Hill. (However, the red-trousered Brooklyn men took a wrong turn and arrived late.) "We pushed at double-quick," wrote one of the Zouaves. "Up, up, not a single enemy in sight, not a shot from his side. Up, up till we gained the top, and then . . ."

Jackson's Rebels held their fire until the Zouaves had swung to the right of Griffin's and Ricketts' batteries. Then the Confederate line stood and delivered a crushing volley. "We literally mowed them down," said a Virginian. Suddenly the air was blue and sulfurous with gun smoke. The Zouaves dropped to the ground in time to escape the second enemy volley. A number of New Yorkers rose on their elbows to return fire, but others, singly and in bewildered groups, broke and ran. The bulk of the regiment

fell back to the rear of the Union batteries.

Confusion enveloped the Confederate line as well. Colonel Arthur Cummings, commanding the 33rd Virginia on Jackson's left, was not sure that the Zouaves in his front were the enemy and ordered his men to hold their fire. He knew that Roberdeau Wheat led a battalion of gaudily uniformed Louisianians. But his doubts vanished a moment later when the New Yorkers sent a belated volley thundering up the slope.

At this point, two companies of Confederate cavalry under Jeb Stuart reached the left end of the battle line and emerged from the woods to assault the New Yorkers' unprotected flank and rear. A brief melee ensued. A few Zouaves used their bayonets to stab passing riders, while the cavalrymen fought back with their sabers or carbines. Soon Stuart drew his command back into the woods. Zouave officers attempted to rally the shaken New Yorkers, intending to lead them back up the slope to support Griffin and Ricketts. But some of the Zouaves fled and others refused to budge.

The Federal batteries had been doing damage all along the Confederate line in front of them. But their own position was jeopardized when Griffin moved two of his guns to an exposed location on Ricketts' right, from which he could enfilade the Confederate line. The gun crews now desperately needed infantry support, but the Zouaves and Marines remained stuck well behind the batteries. Two regiments of Franklin's brigade were also within striking distance in the rear, but they had not been told to advance.

At this point, a violated order and an error of judgment altered the course of the mistake-filled battle. Colonel Cummings of the 33rd Virginia decided to disobey Jackson's order that he simply hold his position. Cummings led his blue-clad regiment forward, heading for the Federal right flank a few hundred yards down the long rise.

Captain Griffin saw the Virginians coming. The two fieldpieces he had placed on the far right were loaded with canister, ideal for use against massed infantry. After brief hesitation caused by the blue uniforms, the captain was about to fire when Major Barry intervened. He was certain that the approaching troops were friendly. "Those are your battery support," he told Griffin, and ordered him not to shoot. "They are Confederates!" Griffin yelled back.

Still, Barry forbade the gunners to fire—until it was too late. When the Virginians had advanced to within 70 yards of the Federal battery, they loosed a devastating volley. It killed a number of men in each of the two Union batteries, wounded Ricketts, slaughtered many horses and stampeded most of the rest. "That was the last of us," Griffin later recalled. As the Virginians swarmed toward the guns, the remaining Zouaves and Marines fled down the slope. Griffin, alone in command and with most of the artillery horses shot, ordered the artillerymen to retire without their guns.

General McDowell and other officers were alarmed at the signs of panic among their infantry. They rode back and forth, desperately trying to re-form the men. Many soldiers did not stop running until they reached Sudley Ford, and the sight of comrades fleeing in fright sent shivers through the fresh Yankee regiments moving up toward the battle line. Some Union outfits were demoralized before they fired their first shot.

The turning point had been reached. Two hours before, McDowell had seen victory in his grasp. Now, at a little after 2 o'clock on this steamy July afternoon, he saw the battle slip beyond control.

Jackson was the first to capitalize on the setback to the enemy batteries. He immediately ordered his brigade to charge. Beauregard committed the units on Jackson's right to the advance as well. Because the enemy was still numerically superior in this sector, the Confederates' momentary advantage had to be exploited quickly, buying time for Johnston to send additional reinforcements.

The next two hours were a confused period of charges and counterattacks. The abandoned guns of Ricketts and Griffin changed hands several times. Losses on both sides mounted steadily as other Federal guns continued to fire and the Confederate batteries answered. "The cannonballs struck all around us," one Virginian later wrote, "the

Colonel Wade Hampton, the organizer, financer and commander of the 600-man Hampton Legion, was reputedly the South's wealthiest planter. He owned some 3,000 slaves—worth perhaps $3 million—and the yearly income from his half-dozen estates approached $200,000.

shells burst at our feet, and the Miniés sung their song of death around our ears." Each time the Confederates swarmed over the hill and struck the Federals a sharp blow, the Yankees recovered and forced the Rebels to retire back over the crest.

The contested Federal fieldpieces were scarcely moved because neither Northern nor Southern troops held dominion over the field long enough to pull them in either direction. At one point, Griffin and men of the 38th New York managed to haul three of the guns toward safety, but just then Jackson's men struck again, with Beauregard himself leading the 5th Virginia and shouting "Give them the bayonet! Give it to them freely!" Griffin once again had to leave his guns—until yet another Federal charge drove the Virginians back.

The battle for the guns raged back and forth. Bartow and his color sergeant, carrying their regimental banner, led the remnants of the 7th Georgia in an all-out counterattack. A bullet caught Bartow near the heart. In his last words he begged his soldiers to hold their banner at all costs: "They have killed me; but boys, *never* give it up."

During the savage fighting, McDowell became so engrossed in riding to and fro along the fighting front, rallying his men, that he lost track of the battle as a whole. He consequently failed to bring up the strong reserves he still possessed. Schenck's brigade spent the entire battle rooted near the Stone Bridge, and Tyler with Keyes's brigade loitered behind Young's Branch through most of the engagement.

McDowell doggedly continued his spendthrift practice of attacking with one brigade at a time; instead of striking with his overwhelming strength, he dribbled away hundreds of lives in modest reverses. Now and then one of the Yankee units actually gained the summit of the hill, only to be thrown back with heavy losses. All the while, troops on both sides were collapsing from heat exhaustion and thirst and from breathing the dust-filled air. Some men died of sunstroke.

Colonel Sherman, as inexperienced as his Yankee compatriots, also began to send his regiments into the fight one at a time, and with the same unhappy results. His 2nd Wisconsin, clad in gray uniforms, advanced to within a few yards of Jackson's right flank before the Confederate soldiers recovered from their confusion and resumed firing.

When the Wisconsin boys were driven back, the 79th New York Highlanders took their place. Again chaos reigned. The Highlanders mistook a Confederate flag for a Union one (the Stars and Bars of the Confederacy resembled the Stars and Stripes from afar, especially on a windless day) and ceased firing. "As we lowered our arms and were about to rally where the banner floated," wrote a Highlander, "we were met by a terrible raking fire, against which we could only stagger." The Highlanders fell back down the hill. "As we passed down we saw our Colonel lying still in the hands of Death."

The colonel was James Cameron. A few miles away, listening to the roar of the battle, stood his brother, Secretary of War Simon Cameron.

The Federal commanders were wasting their regiments so prodigally that their lines soon became a jumble of fragmented units, and whatever semblance of organization remained was threatening to disintegrate at any moment. At about 3:45 p.m. the last unbloodied brigade was committed to the battle—three regiments from Maine and

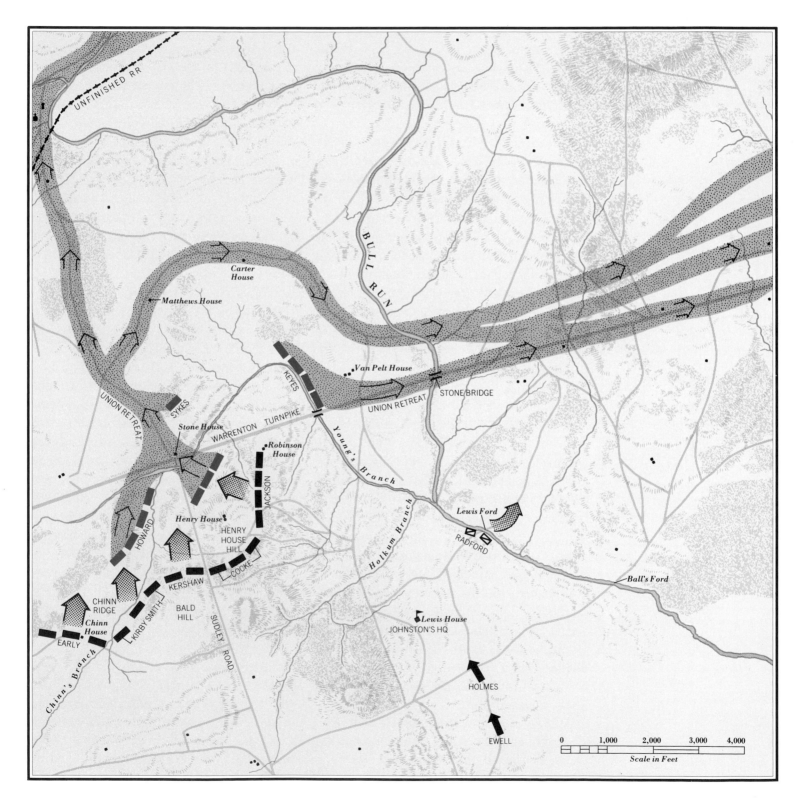

Starting the Federal rout, the Confederate brigades of General Edmund Kirby Smith and Colonel Jubal A. Early arrived to hammer Colonel Oliver O. Howard's brigade, the last fresh Union unit. Elsewhere, Union troops began to leave the field in disorder, some men fleeing by way of Sudley Ford, others taking the shorter route across the Stone Bridge. General Beauregard ordered a full-scale Confederate attack.

one from Vermont, commanded by Colonel Oliver Howard. But Howard's command had made the long march via Sudley Ford during the hottest part of the day with heavy field packs and empty canteens, and they were exhausted. They tried to obey McDowell's order to deploy at a run, but many failed. "Our men began to fall out and could not go any farther," a Maine private said. "I think at least one quarter of the men fell out before we got to the battlefield."

Howard formed his brigade in two lines on the right of the Federal position and gave the order to attack. His first line met a hail of fire. Orders could not be heard above the din, and the men were unnerved to see bloodied Federals from earlier assaults fleeing in terror. Like the troops in many frightened units before them, some of Howard's soldiers became disoriented and fired their weapons into the air. Many were unable to fire at all; they had neglected to put a percussion cap on the nipple at the rifle's breach. Some of those who forgot to use a percussion cap failed to notice that the rifle had not fired and kept ramming more charges home. A few men even forgot to remove their ramrods from the barrels before firing and sent them sailing over the field like arrows.

Howard's first line was badly mauled, so the colonel went back down the slope to bring up his second line. This line in turn was met by devastating blasts from the Confederate artillery and volleys from fresh Confederate troops on their right flank. Groups of Maine Volunteers soon began to break for the rear. Howard had no alternative but to order all his men to retreat. They broke and fled, stopping only after they were back across Young's Branch.

Those fresh Confederate brigades now reaching the battle were just in time to strike telling blows. One such unit was the brigade commanded by Brigadier General Edmund Kirby Smith. After arriving at Manassas Junction around 12:30, Smith had rapidly formed his troops and quick-marched them along roads choked with dust and strewn with wounded men and stragglers. "Our pulses beat more quickly than our feet," wrote a man in the brigade, "the sounds of battle waxing nearer and nearer every moment." When Smith reached Portici, General Johnston met him and gave him simple orders. "Take them to the front," he said. "Go where the fire is hottest."

At about 4 p.m. Smith led his men past the southern slope of Henry House Hill and off toward the left. Colonel Howard's Union brigade seemed to be re-forming there for another attack, and Colonel Joseph B. Kershaw, commanding the 2nd South Carolina of Bonham's brigade, directed Smith's attention to the threat. Moments later a volley from Howard's men came whistling up the hill; a bullet struck Smith in the chest and knocked him out of the battle. The command of the Rebel brigade devolved on Colonel Arnold Elzey of the 1st Maryland. Determined to earn the rank and sword belt of a Confederate general, Elzey said that he would end this day with "a yellow sash or six feet of ground." Elzey was later promoted to brigadier general—retroactive to the very day of the battle.

Moving the brigade quietly through thick woods west of Henry House Hill, Elzey suddenly struck the exposed right flank of Colonel Howard's exhausted, jittery troops. The attack put Howard's men to rout, and the entire right wing of McDowell's army began to crumble. Joining Elzey in the at-

Sword-waving Colonel Louis Blenker signals his New York volunteers to open fire on Confederate cavalry riding in hot pursuit of the retreating Union troops (*far left*). Refusing to be panicked by the Federal rout, Blenker's brigade held its ground just south of Centreville.

tack was the brigade of Colonel Jubal Early.

The Federals were giving way fast. "A panic had seized all the troops in sight," Colonel Howard said. Union soldiers were running about in confusion, throwing away their guns, shaking off their heavy equipment and shouting, "The enemy is upon us! We shall all be taken!"

Beauregard sensed that the decisive moment was at hand, and he boldly led his entire line forward in an attack. McDowell's adjutant, Captain James Fry, later reported, "The men seemed to be seized simultaneously by the conviction that it was no use to do anything more and they might as well start home." They had fought remarkably well for inexperienced summer soldiers, but now

they had had enough. The whole Yankee line fell apart and went to the rear.

The retreat began about 4:30. McDowell later recalled painfully that "the plain was covered with retreating troops, and they seemed to infect those with whom they came in contact. The retreat soon became a rout, and this soon degenerated still further into a panic." The best that McDowell could do was attempt to cover the withdrawal of his army against enemy pursuit. He sent Major George Sykes's battalion of hard-bitten Regular Army infantry to the vulnerable Union right to cover the stampede from the battlefield. The rest of his force was beyond control. Some of the men ran with crazed fear toward Sudley Ford or Centreville. Most, too weary to run, simply shambled off the field, discarding their gear as they went.

Beauregard sent one unit after another in pursuit of the fleeing enemy. Early went directly after Howard's brigade while Stuart and his horsemen followed the main body of the Federals. The cavalrymen soon had to stop, however; they had taken so many prisoners that they could no longer advance. Other cavalry detachments crossed Bull Run south of the Stone Bridge in the hope of getting behind Hunter's and Heintzelman's fleeing men before they completed their wide swing via Sudley Ford back to the Warrenton Turnpike. But while these horsemen were advancing, Beauregard heard a rumor that Yankee units had been seen threatening Union Mills, far to his right. Fearing another attack, he postponed a full-scale pursuit until the rumor was proved false. By then the

Union troops had fled too far to be caught.

Johnston, meanwhile, made another attempt to head off the defeated Federals, ordering Longstreet and Bonham to cross Bull Run at Mitchell's and Blackburn's Fords and advance on Centreville. Should they reach the village before McDowell's men did, they would cut the main escape route to Washington. But the Union Mills rumor delayed Longstreet and Bonham also, and then they were stopped by Colonel Israel Richardson's fresh Federal brigade, stationed south of Centreville to block access to the town. These Yankees showed no inclination to stand aside, so the two Confederate brigades at last returned to Bull Run.

In fact, the Confederates were just as worn out as the Federals. Even the brigades that had not fought had been marching most of the day in the heat, and by the time the rout began there was not enough daylight left for an effective pursuit, even with fresh troops. Beauregard officially called off the chase shortly after 7 o'clock. Only a squadron of Colonel R.C.W. Radford's 30th Virginia Cavalry, which had been held in reserve, actually clashed with the fleeing Federals. The cavalrymen charged wildly into the rear guard of Erasmus Keyes's brigade just west of the Cub Run bridge on the Warrenton Turnpike. A fierce melee followed, but in the end the Virginians were driven off by a battery of Regular Army artillery.

The most damage was done by Captain Delaware Kemper's Virginia battery, which closed to within range of the same Cub Run bridge. Kemper offered the honor of firing the first shot to an elderly civilian guest, the famed secessionist agitator Edmund Ruffin, who had fired one of the first shots at Fort Sumter. Ruffin jerked the lanyard and sent a

The punctured pages of a pocket-sized New Testament show where the book stopped a bullet that would otherwise have killed Private A. P. Hubbard of the 4th South Carolina during the Bull Run battle. This was the first of many Bibles that saved the lives of Civil War soldiers.

perfectly aimed shell to the middle of the bridge. The explosion overturned a wagon, which blocked the span just as two Federal columns were converging on it. Abandoning arms, wagons and anything else that might slow their flight, the Yankees waded across the stream to continue their race for Centreville. That was the last stroke. The battle was done, the day a Southern triumph.

Nor did the Confederate forces attempt a pursuit the following day. President Davis, who had reached the battlefield from Richmond in time to witness the rout, agreed with General Johnston that the troops, weary and hungry, with little food and less ammunition, were in no shape to undertake forced marches. In addition, a drenching rain started to fall during the night and continued into July 22, turning the roads into quagmires. Davis contented himself with sending an exultant telegram to his capital, where everyone went wild with jubilation over the news of victory.

On the Federal side, General McDowell managed to re-form enough of his army to erect a defensive line anchored on his reserves at Centreville, but it was obvious to him and his officers that they could not remain there. Half the army was still streaming in panic toward Washington and would not stop before crossing the Potomac. McDowell had no choice but to follow, and on July 22 the remainder of his command marched glumly back to Alexandria. The battle had cost the army its spirit, and McDowell had good reason to think that it would soon cost him his command.

The Yankees' return to Washington was doleful, almost funereal. Walt Whitman, then a reporter for the Brooklyn *Standard*, jotted down staccato, impressionistic notes:

"The defeated troops commenced pouring into Washington over the Long Bridge at daylight on Monday, 22nd—day drizzling all through with rain . . . their clothes all saturated with the clay-powder filling the air—stirr'd up everywhere on the dry roads and trodden fields by the regiments, swarming wagons, artillery, etc.—all the men with this coating of murk and sweat and rain, now recoiling back, pouring over the Long Bridge—a horrible march of 20 miles, returning to Washington baffled, humiliated, panic-struck. Where are the vaunts, and the proud boasts with which you went forth? Where are your banners, and your bands of music, and your ropes to bring back your prisoners?

"The sun rises, but shines not. The men appear, at first sparsely and shame-faced enough, then thicker, in the streets of Washington—appear in Pennsylvania Avenue, and on the steps and basement entrances. They come along in disorderly mobs, some in squads, stragglers, companies. During the forenoon, Washington gets all over motley with these defeated soldiers—queer-looking objects, strange eyes and faces, drench'd (the steady rain drizzles on all day) and fearfully worn, hungry, haggard, blister'd in the feet. Good people (but not over-many of them either) hurry up something for their grub. They put wash-kettles on the fire, for soup, for coffee. They set tables on the sidewalks—wagonloads of bread are purchas'd, swiftly cut into stout chunks. Here are two aged ladies, beautiful, . . . they stand with store of eating and drink at an improvis'd table of rough plank, and give food, and have the store replenish'd from their house every half-hour all that day; and there in the rain

Planks in a swampy area of the Bull Run battlefield mark the graves of Union troops killed there in July 1861. This photograph was taken eight months later, after the Confederates had abandoned the Bull Run line. When Union troops marched in unopposed, they found that most of their dead comrades had been hastily piled into mass graves.

151

they stand, active, silent, white-hair'd, and give food, though the tears stream down their cheeks almost without intermission, the whole time.

"Amid the deep excitement, crowds and motion, and desperate eagerness, it seems strange to see many, very many, of the soldiers sleeping—in the midst of all sleeping sound. They drop down anywhere, on the steps of houses, up close by the basements or fences, on the sidewalk, aside on some vacant lot, and deeply sleep. A poor 17- or 18-year-old boy lies there, on the stoop of a grand house; he sleeps so calmly, so profoundly. Some clutch their muskets firmly even in sleep. Some in squads; comrades, brothers, close together—and on them, as they lay, sulkily drips the rain."

It had been a surprisingly vicious battle, considering that for all but a few it was the awkward first fight of their lives. To be sure, many had panicked and run at the first shots. But many more had stood and fought hard and contributed to casualties that were shockingly high. The Confederates suffered 387 killed, 1,582 wounded and 13 missing, and unreported injuries probably swelled the total casualties to 2,000. Fully one fourth of those came from Jackson's brigade. Though the Virginians had been slow getting into the fight, they then stayed at the vortex of the battle. But for Jackson's skillful, tenacious defense, Beauregard's army would very likely have been the one that fled the scene.

It was Jackson, Bee, Bartow and Evans who had made the difference. And while the reverent Jackson attributed the victory to the Almighty, Nathan Evans placed the responsibility a bit closer to home. There was "no use for other generals to brag about what

they did in the battle," he said. According to a staff officer, Evans said that he had "inaugurated that fight, and he and General Bee fought it through, and he and Bee whipped the fight before any reinforcements came."

Amid the Confederate euphoria there was grief over the loss of Bee, Bartow and other officers, and all too soon internecine squabbles began to tarnish some of the living heroes. Beauregard, who to some extent had made amends for his confused attack plans and weak tactical leadership by his courage under fire, was cocky now, and he began to bedevil President Davis over rank and promotion; within weeks the two had become bitter enemies. Johnston, who felt that he had not received proper recognition for his contribution to the victory, would come to despise them both. Though he had incautiously made himself partner to Beauregard's poor planning and shaky command decisions, Johnston too had redeemed himself by realizing that the left flank was in danger and by displaying strong staff work in deploying reinforcements as they arrived on the battlefield. Despite the disappointing performance of the two top commanders, and despite the losses among their chief subordinates, the Confederate Army came out of the battle with a solid nucleus of capable leaders at the brigade and regiment level.

"It's damned bad" was Lincoln's comment when he heard the first news of the beating that McDowell had suffered. It was worse when Lincoln and his military leaders counted their losses. At least 470 were dead, 1,071 more were wounded and 1,793—the equivalent of nearly two regiments—were missing and presumed captured or killed, raising the total to more than 3,000.

No one in the Army appeared to blame

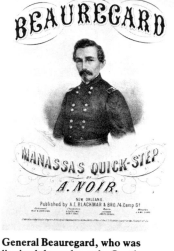

General Beauregard, who was lionized throughout the South as the hero of both Fort Sumter and the Battle of Bull Run ("Manassas" to Southerners), adorns the sheet music of a song composed in his honor. The title was a triple pun: "Quick-step" was a dance, a faster-than-normal army march, and a sly reference to the unseemly speed with which the Union troops fled the battlefield.

Battle Art and Fictitious Victories

The furious scene below, purportedly depicting an incident in the Bull Run battle, appeared shortly afterward, marking the start of a genre of Civil War battle art. A torrent of such works flowed from the sketch pads of artist-correspondents who followed the armies; their illustrations for newspapers and magazines gave the public pictures that could not be provided by the camera, which was still in its infancy and unable to capture action. Some pictures were superb as reportage and as art—for example, the works of Alfred Waud and Winslow Homer. Others were second-rate as art but thoroughly accurate in portraying battles. And still others—such as the print shown here, published by the firm of Currier and Ives in 1861—were sorely lacking in both artistic and reportorial merit.

This picture represents—according to its title—"The Gallant Charge of the Zouaves and Defeat of the Rebel Black Horse Cavalry." The 11th New York Fire Zouaves did in fact clash with Confederate horsemen at Bull Run, but they neither charged nor defeated them; instead the New Yorkers were demoralized. And the Zouaves' enemy was Jeb Stuart's 1st Virginia Cavalry, not the Black Horse Troop of the 4th Virginia.

Distortions like this were sometimes ordered by editors or publishers; they told the engravers to doctor the artists' sketches to satisfy the public demand for heroes, victories and grand-scale battles. But the artists themselves were often at fault. Some illustrated mistaken or boastful soldiers' tales. Others simply used their imaginations. And the anonymous limner of the Zouaves' fictitious victory may well have illustrated a wildly inaccurate report in *The New York Times* of July 24, 1861. "The Zouaves," proclaimed the *Times,* "literally decimated the Black Horse Cavalry" in "hand-to-hand conflict."

Locked in misrepresented combat, Zouaves in trousers of the wrong color (red instead of blue) bayonet Rebels in coats of the wrong style (Union cavalry).

Union soldiers captured at Bull Run mark time in the courtyard of Castle Pinckney in Charleston Harbor while their youthful guards sprawl on the parapet above. The prisoners, 156 members of New York and Michigan regiments, had been dispatched to the island fortress after proving themselves too troublesome to be held in a Richmond prison.

McDowell personally for the defeat. Years later even the critical Sherman, by then the United States Army's commanding general, would credit McDowell with "one of the best-planned battles of the War." The Federal forces lost, said Sherman, because it was also "one of the worst-fought." In fact, the Federal plan had been much more sound than Beauregard's clumsy strategy. But the Union army, with rare exceptions, had been atrociously led. A disillusioned New Hampshire soldier put the bitter truth succinctly: "Every order was a blunder and every movement a failure."

Among civilians, many Northerners—no doubt including some who had exhorted Lincoln to hurry into battle—now blamed the President for forcing McDowell to fight before his army was ready. A Congressional investigation later cleared McDowell of blame for the disaster. He and many other culpable, incapable Union officers would retain enough credit to mismanage other battles. But there would be better things to come from Union officers who had not discredited themselves, or whose conduct during the battle had shone brightly in the gloom of defeat. These officers—men such as Griffin, Ricketts, Richardson and Sherman—would benefit no little from the hard lessons they had learned along Bull Run.

One lesson and one course of remedial action were immediately clear to Lincoln, his Cabinet and General Winfield Scott: The shattered Federal army must be pieced together again fast, and by a general other than McDowell. On July 25, just four days after the battle, Scott looked off to the West to a general who had given the Union victories—not great ones, to be sure, but victories none-theless. Scott called George B. McClellan east and put him in command of the Union armies around Washington.

Other lessons were learned from the Battle of Bull Run (so called by Northerners, who usually named battles after the nearest geographical feature; Southerners called it the Battle of Manassas and would persist in naming battles after the nearest town). Before Bull Run, many soldiers on both sides had written and spoken romantic twaddle about military service, in much the same vein as a giddy volunteer from New York: "Nothing men can do—except picnics, with ladies in straw hats and flowers—is so picturesque as soldiering." After Bull Run, a soldier who fought there grimly confessed: "I had a dim notion about the 'romance' of a soldier's life. I have bravely got over it since."

Before Bull Run, many people on both sides expected the War to be a short one, and cynics even said that the powerful Northern bankers and big Southern planters would not permit fighting to interrupt their normal business for long. But the confusion of the battle suggested that both sides would take some time to turn their amateur armies into efficient fighting forces, and the men who were killed at Bull Run sealed in blood the commitment of both sides to fight the War through to an uncompromised decision.

A lust to avenge Bull Run soon inspirited the depressed Federal troops in their camps around Washington. Said a Yankee soldier: "We shall flog these scoundrels and traitors all the more bitterly for it before we are done with them." Now a new determination to win moved Federals and Confederates to write home the same pledge: "I shall see the thing played out or die in the attempt."

"Seeing the Elephant"

The soldiers who fought their first battle at Bull Run on July 21, 1861, were shocked—like soldiers in every war—to discover the savagery of combat. To express their reaction to the experience, they adopted a phrase from farm boys who, after attending a traveling circus, spoke with awe of "seeing the elephant." Some of their feelings are captured on these pages in their words and in artists' renderings of critical moments in the daylong battle.

To McHenry Howard of the 1st Mary-land Infantry, the baptism of fire at Bull Run came "as if in a dream, the whole thing was so sudden, unexpected and novel." A private in the 8th Georgia wrote, "The whole air sounded as though a large aeolian harp was hung over, around and about us." Another Southerner compared the duel of enemy guns to "two mailed giants hammering each other with huge battle axes."

In this first great clash of the War, officers who were as inexperienced as their men found it next to impossible to

Colonel Ambrose Burnside's brigade joins battle with Colonel Nathan Evans' Confederates on Matthews Hill at 9:45 a.m. on July 21. The regiments advancing in

maintain discipline. Inexplicably, an entire Confederate regiment broke ranks in midcharge and went off to pick blackberries. Captain Charles Griffin of the 5th U.S. Artillery reported that "a great many of our regiments turned right off the field as they delivered their fire. They went right off as a crowd would walking the street—every man for himself, with no organization whatever." Another Union officer, who had repeatedly shouted orders to his men, said that "they seemed to be paralyzed, standing with their eyes and mouths wide open, and did not seem to hear me."

Troops on both sides were victimized by their lack of physical and mental preparation. Dozens of men, wearing heavy woolen uniforms, burdened with gear and short on water, collapsed of sunstroke in the midsummer heat. Even the soldiers' humane instincts worked against them: Scores of men left their units in the lurch to help casualties. "The sufferings of the wounded," wrote an officer of the 11th Massachusetts, "moved the hearts of men who had not by long experience become callous to the sight of human agony."

In the final reckoning, there was not much difference between the Confederates and the Federals in fighting prowess. In such balanced circumstances, resolution alone was bound to count heavily, and the Confederates at Bull Run were unshakably resolved. Said one Rebel: "The truth is, we were so unused to a fight and determined on victory, that we never dreamed of retiring."

line past the Matthews house (*left*) are the 2nd Rhode Island, the 1st Rhode Island and the 71st New York.

"There stands Jackson like a stone wall!   Rally behind the Virginians!"

BRIGADIER GENERAL BARNARD E. BEE, C.S.A.

Apparently winning the day, Union forces at 2 p.m. drive the shattered brigades of Bee, Bartow and Evans across the Warrenton Turnpike, past the Robinson house and

up Henry House Hill. But success eluded the Federals as the Confederates, urged on by General Bee, made a last stand behind Thomas J. Jackson's Virginians (*inset*).

> *"I leaned down from the saddle, rammed the muzzle of the carbine into the stomach of my man and pulled the trigger. He tried to get his bayonet up to meet me; but he was too slow, for the carbine blew a hole as big as my arm clear through him."*

ADJUTANT WILLIAM W. BLACKFORD, 1ST VIRGINIA CAVALRY

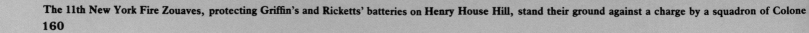

The 11th New York Fire Zouaves, protecting Griffin's and Ricketts' batteries on Henry House Hill, stand their ground against a charge by a squadron of Colone

Jeb Stuart's 1st Virginia Cavalry. Although the Fire Zouaves managed to repulse the attack, they were left shaken and demoralized.

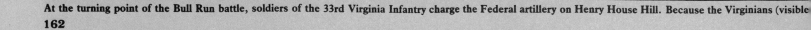

> *"I saw some troops in front of us. Down came their rifles and muskets, and probably there never was such a destructive fire for a few minutes. The Marines and Zouaves seemed to be struck with such astonishment that they could not do anything."*

FIRST LIEUTENANT WILLIAM W. AVERELL, 3RD U.S. CAVALRY

At the turning point of the Bull Run battle, soldiers of the 33rd Virginia Infantry charge the Federal artillery on Henry House Hill. Because the Virginians (visible

162

through the smoke at right) wore blue uniforms, Captain Charles Griffin of the Federal artillery was mistakenly instructed to hold his fire, and disaster followed.

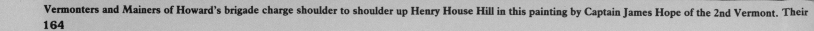

> *"The enemy's battery on the left, and the one on the right, with the showers of musket balls from the front, made it rather warm work for new men."*
>
> COLONEL OLIVER O. HOWARD, 3RD MAINE INFANTRY

Vermonters and Mainers of Howard's brigade charge shoulder to shoulder up Henry House Hill in this painting by Captain James Hope of the 2nd Vermont. Their

assault was the last of several Union efforts to recapture guns lost hours before. General E. Kirby Smith's Confederates soon flanked and routed the New Englanders.

"Bidding those of my staff and escort raise a loud cheer, I dispatched orders to go forward in a common charge. Before the full advance of the Confederate ranks the enemy's whole line irretrievably broke, fleeing across Bull Run by every available direction."

GENERAL P.G.T. BEAUREGARD, C.S.A.

Mounting a climactic counterattack, General Beauregard urges his men forward to victory against crumbling Federal resistance. The Confederate drive, executed

between 4 and 5 p.m., was made possible by the arrival of General Joseph E. Johnston's fresh troops from the Shenandoah Valley.

Retreating in panic, disorganized Union troops crowd the roads leading east from Bull Run to Centreville and Washington, D.C. In this watercolor by William Trego,

"*Cavalry horses without riders, wrecked baggage wagons and pieces of artillery drawn by six horses without drivers, flying at their utmost speed and whacking against other vehicles, produced a noise like a hurricane at sea.*"

COLONEL ERASMUS D. KEYES, 11TH U.S. INFANTRY

a soldier of the 14th Brooklyn Chasseurs flees beside stampeding commissary wagons in what became known as "the great skedaddle."

NEW FAIRFIELD FREE PUBLIC LIBRARY · NEW FAIRFIELD, CT.

ACKNOWLEDGMENTS

The editors thank the following individuals and institutions for their help in the preparation of the Civil War series:

Alabama: Birmingham—Birmingham Museum of Art. Mobile—Jay P. Altmayer; The First National Bank of Mobile; Caldwell Delaney, The Museum of the City of Mobile; R. Erwin Neville. Montgomery—Alabama Department of Archives and History; First White House of the Confederacy. Northport—Mrs. Ellis F. Cannon. Tuscaloosa—William Stanley Hoole Special Collections, University of Alabama Library; Jack Warner.

Arizona: Mesa—Jeffrey N. Brown.

Arkansas: Jonesboro—Arkansas State University Museum. Little Rock—Robert Serio, The Old State House.

California: San Marino—Carey Bliss, Alan Jetsie, Brita Mack, Harriet McLoone, Virginia Reuner, Huntingdon Library. Santa Barbara—Chris Brun, University of California, Special Collections.

Connecticut: Bridgeport—Bridgeport Public Library. Fairfield—Tom Lopiano Jr. Hartford—Connecticut State Library. New Haven—Yale University Library. New Milford—Norm Flayderman. Westport—William Gladstone, Ed Vebell.

Delaware: Wilmington—Historical Society of Delaware.

Florida: Bradenton—South Florida Museum. Pensacola—John C. Pace Library, University of West Florida; Pensacola Historical Museum; T. T. Wentworth Jr. Museum; West Florida Museum of History. Tallahassee—Florida State Archives; Florida State Photo Archives; Florida State University Library; Museum of Florida History.

Georgia: Athens—Robert M. Willingham Jr., University of Georgia Libraries, Special Collections; Charles East, University of Georgia Press. Atlanta—Atlanta Historical Society; Tom Dickey; Beverly M. DuBose Jr.; William Erquitt; Gail Miller, Georgia Department of Archives and History; Robert W. Woodruff Library, Special Collections, Emory University. Augusta—Augusta-Richmond County Museum. Crawfordsville—The Confederate Museum, Alexander H. Stephens Memorial. Richmond Hill—Fort McAllister. St. Simons Island—Museum of Coastal History. Savannah—Anthony R. Dees, Georgia Historical Society; United Daughters of the Confederac Collection. Washington—Washington-Wilkes Historical Collections.

Illinois: Chicago—Joseph B. Zywicki, Chicago Historical Society. Springfield—Camp Lincoln; Rodger D. Bridges, James Hickey, Mariana James Munyer, Illinois State Historical Library, Old State Capitol. Wheaton—Du Page County Historical Museum.

Indiana: Bloomington — The Lilly Library, Indiana University. Fort Wayne — Mark E. Neely Jr., Louis A. Warren Lincoln Library and Museum. Indianapolis — The Children's Museum; Indiana Historical Society; Indiana State Library; Indiana War Memorials Commission.

Iowa: Des Moines—Iowa State Historical Society, Museum and Archives Division.

Kansas: Topeka—Kansas State Historical Society.

Kentucky: Frankfort—Linda Anderson, Kentucky Historical Society; Nicky Hughes, Kentucky Military History Museum.

Louisiana: Baton Rouge—H. Parrott Bacot, Anglo-American Art Museum, Louisiana State University; Beth Benton; Fred G. Benton Jr.; Dr. Edward Boagni; Shelby Gilley; M. Stone Miller, Main Library, Louisiana State University; Bill Moore. Natchitoches—Dr. John Price, Dr. Carol Wells, Louisiana Archives, Northwestern University. New Orleans—Barnard Eble, Pat Eymard, Confederate Memorial Hall; Charles Dufour; W. E. Groves; Patricia McWhorter, Kenneth T. Urquhart, The Historic New Orleans Collection; Mary B. Oalmann, Colonel Francis E. Thomas, Jackson Barracks; George E. Jordan; Vaughn Glasgow, Louisiana State Museum; Wilbur E. Meneray, Tulane University Library.

Maine: Augusta—Sylvia Sherman, Maine State Archives; Jane Radcliffe, Maine State Museum. Brunswick—The Hawthorne Longfellow Library; Elizabeth Copeland, Pejepscot Historical Society. Portland—Elizabeth Hamill, Maine Historical Society.

Maryland: Annapolis—Sigrid H. Trumpy, Alexandra H. Welsh, The Beverley R. Robinson Collection, The United States Naval Academy Museum; James W. Cheevers, The United States Naval Academy Museum. Baltimore—Donna Ellis, Paula Velthuys, Maryland Historical Society. Bethesda—Lucy Keister, National Library of Medicine. Cumberland—Allegany Historical Society, Inc.

Massachusetts: Boston—Boston Public Library, Print Department and Rare Book Room; Commonwealth of Massachusetts, State Library; Francis A. Countway Library, Harvard Medical School; Craig W. C. Brown, First Corps of Cadets Military Museum; Massachusetts State House; Cynthia English, Sally Pearce, Library of the Boston Athenaeum; Massachusetts Historical Society; Museum of Fine Arts; Society for the Preservation of New England Antiquities; James Stamatelos. Cambridge — Houghton Library, Harvard University; The Arthur and Elizabeth Schlesinger Library, Radcliffe College, Ipswich — Lewis Joslyn. Marblehead — Marblehead Historical Society. Newburyport — Historical Society of Old Newbury. Northampton — The Sophia Smith Collection, Smith College. Salem — Essex Institute; Peabody Museum. Springfield — Springfield Armory National Historic Site. Worcester — Higgins Armory; Worcester Art Museum; Worcester Historical Society.

Michigan: Ann Arbor—Mary Jo Pugh, Bentley Historical Library; John Dann, The William L. Clements Library, The University of Michigan. Detroit—Thomas Featherstone, Archives of Labor and Urban Affairs, Walter P. Reuther Library, Wayne State University; Alice Cook Dalligan, Noel VanGorden, Burton Historical Collection, Detroit Public Library; Anita D. McCandless, Detroit Historical Museum; William P. Phenix, Historic Fort Wayne. East Lansing—Frederick L. Honhart, University Archives, Historical Collections, Michigan State University; William J. Prince. Kalamazoo—James Brady Jr., Paul DeHaan; Patricia Gordon Michael, Mary Lou Stewart, Kalamazoo Public Museum. Lansing—Ruby Rogers, Michigan Historical Museum, Michigan Department of State; John C. Curry State Archives, Michigan Department of State; Karl Rommel.

Minnesota: St. Paul—Minnesota Historical Society.

Mississippi: Clinton—Bill Wright. Jackson—Department of Archives and History; Patricia Carr Black, State Historical Museum. Natchez—The Historic Natchez Foundation; William Stewart. Vicksburg—Gordon A. Cotton, Old Courthouse Museum; Vicksburg National Military Park.

Missouri: Columbia—State of Missouri Historical Society; Western Manuscript Collection, University of Missouri. Jefferson City—Missouri Department of Natural Resources; Missouri State Museum. St. Louis—Missouri Historical Society.

New Hampshire: Concord—Mary Rose Boswell, New Hampshire Historical Society.

New Jersey: Merchantville—C. Paul Loane. Newark—Alan Frazer, The New Jersey Historical Society. Pittstown—John Kuhl. Ridgefield—Val J. Forgett. Woodbury—Edith Hoelle, Gloucester County Historical Society.

New York: Albany—Gene Deaton, The Military Museum, State of New York Division of Military and Naval Affairs; Joseph Meany, Robert Mulligan, New York State Museum. Fishers—J. Sheldon Fisher, Valentown Museum. Hudson—American Museum of Firefighting; D.A.R. Museum. New York—The New-York Historical Society; Colonel Benjamin P. Fowler, USAF (Retired), Lieutenant William H. Schmidt, Veterans of the 7th New York. Peekskill—Memorial Museum of the Field Library. Rochester—Janice Wass, Rochester Museum and Science Center. Troy—The Rensselaer County Historical Society. West Point—Marie Capps, U.S. Military Academy Library; Michael E. Moss, West Point Museum.

North Carolina: Chapel Hill—Richard Shrader, Southern Historical Collection, University of North Carolina Library. Durham—Robert Byrd, William Erwin, Ellen Gartell, Dr. Mattie Russell, William Perkins Library, Duke University. Raleigh—Dick Lankford, Division of Archives and Records; Keith Strawn, North Carolina Department of Cultural Resources. Wilmington—Susan A. Krause, Bill Reaves, Janet Seapker, New Hanover County Museum.

Ohio: Cincinnati—Cincinnati Historical Society; First National Bank. Cleveland—James B. Casey, Western Reserve Historical Society. Columbus—Ohio Historical Society. Coolville—Larry M. Strayer. Fremont—Rutherford B. Hayes Presidential Center. Hudson—T. Price Gibson; Thomas L. Vince, Hudson Library and Historical Society. Massillon—Margy Vogt, Massillon Museum. Mechanicsburg—Champaign County Historical Society.

Pennsylvania: Allentown—Lehigh County Historical Society. Carlisle—Randy Hackenburg, Dr. Richard Sommers, Michael S. Winey, Military History Institute. Gettysburg—D. Mark Katz. Gladwyne—Terry O'Leary. Harrisburg—Bruce Bazelon, William Penn Memorial Museum. Kittanning—Ronn Palm. Milford—Pike County Historical Society. North East—Irwin Rider. Philadelphia—Sandra Gross, Atwater Kent Museum; Free Library of Philadelphia; The Historical Society of Pennsylvania; Manuel Kean, Kean Archives; The Library Company of Philadelphia; Craig Nannos, First Regiment, Pennsylvania National Guard Armory and Museum; Philadelphia Maritime Museum; Russ A. Pritchard; The War Library and Museum of the Military Order of the Loyal Legion of the United States. Whitehall—Harry Roach, *Military Images Magazine.*

Rhode Island: Newport—Colonel James V. Coleman, Newport Artillery Company Armory. Providence—Richard B. Harrington, Anne S. K. Brown Military Collection; Jennifer B. Lee, John Hay Library, Brown University; Brigadier General John W. Kiely, Office of the Adjutant General; Providence Public Library; Joyce M. Botelho, Tom G. Brennan, The Rhode Island Historical Society Library and Museum.

South Carolina: Beaufort—June Berry, Beaufort Museum; Joel Martin. Charleston—Charleston Museum; Archives, The Citadel; Confederate Museum; Warren Ripley, *The Evening Post;* Martha Severns, Gibbes Art Gallery; Harlan Greene, South Carolina Historical Society; Julian V. Brandt III, Washington Light Infantry. Columbia—Fort Jackson Museum; Dr. Francis Lord; Laverne Watson, South Carolina Confederate Relic Room and Museum; Charles Gay, Alan Stokes, South Caroliniana Library, University of South Carolina; University of South Carolina McKissick Museums. Spartanburg—Robert M. Hicklin Jr. Sullivan's Island—David Ruth, Forts Moultrie and Sumter. Union—Dr. Lloyd Sutherland; Union County Museum.

Tennessee: Chattanooga—Chattanooga Museum of Regional History. Dover—Fort Donelson National Military Park. Franklin—Carter House. Greeneville—Andrew Johnson Historic Site. Harrogate—Edgar G. Archer, Abraham Lincoln Library and Museum, Lincoln Memorial University. Knoxville—Confederate Memorial Hall "Bleak House." Memphis—Eleanor McKay, Mississippi Valley Collection of Memphis State University; Nashville—Belmont Mansion; Fisk University Library Special Collections; Sarah and C. William Green-Devon Farm; Nashville Room, Public Library of Nashville and Davidson County; Herb Peck Jr.; Tennessee Historical Society; Tennessee State Library and Archives; Tennessee State Museum.

Texas: Austin—Eugene Barker Library, University of Texas; Confederate Museum; Texas State Archives.

Vermont: Bennington — Ruth Levin, Bennington Museum. Montpelier — Mary Pat Johnson, Vermont Historical Society; Philip Elwart, Vermont Museum.

Virginia: Alexandria — Wanda Dowell, Fort Ward Park; Boyhood Home of Robert E. Lee; Lee-Fendall House; Lloyd House, Alexandria Library. Arlington — Agnes Mullix, Arlington House, The Robert E. Lee Memorial. Fort Belvoir — John M. Dervan, U.S. Army Engineer Museum. Fort Monroe — R. Cody Phillips, The Casemate Museum, Department of the Army. Fredericksburg — Robert Krick, Fredericksburg/Spotsylvania National Military Park. Lexington — Robert C. Peniston, Lee Chapel Museum, Washington and Lee University; Barbara Crawford, Stonewall Jackson House; Virginia Military Institute Library; June F. Cunningham, Virginia Military Institute Museum; Washington and Lee University Library. Manassas — James Burgess, Manassas National Battlefield Park. Marion — Marion-Smyth County Historical and Museum Society, Inc. New Market — James G. Geary, New Market Battlefield Park. Newport News — Lois Oglesby, Charlotte Valentine, The Mariners Museum; John V. Quarstein, The War Memorial Museum of Virginia. Petersburg — Christopher M. Calkins, Petersburg National Battlefield Park. Portsmouth — Alice C. Hanes, Portsmouth Naval Shipyard Museum. Quantico — Marine Corps Historical Center. Richmond — Dr. Edward Campbell Jr., Cathy Carlson, The Museum of the Confederacy; Sarah Shields, Valentine Museum; Rebecca Perrine, Virginia Historical Society; Virginia State Library. Williamsburg — Margaret Cook, Earl Gregg Swem Library, The College of William and Mary.

Washington, D.C.: Oliver Jenson, Jerry L. Kearns, Bernard F. Riley, Library of Congress, Prints and Photographs Division; Washingtoniana Division, Martin Luther King Library; James H. Trimble, Audio-Visual Archives, Still Pictures Branch, National Archives and Record Service; National Portrait Gallery; Smithsonian Institution; Anne-Imelda Radice, Curator for the Architect of the U.S. Capitol.

West Virginia: Harpers Ferry—Dennis E. Frye, Harpers Ferry National Historical Park; Fonda Thomsen, National Park Service, Harpers Ferry Center; Morgantown—Ginger Bevard, West Virginia and Regional History Collection, West Virginia University. Weston—Jackson's Mill Museum.

Wisconsin: Madison—Dr. Richard Zeitlin, G.A.R. Memorial Hall Museum; State Historical Society of Wisconsin. Milwaukee—Howard Madaus, Milwaukee Public Museum; Gary S. Pagel.

The index for this book was prepared by Nicholas J. Anthony.

BIBLIOGRAPHY

Books

Albaugh, William A., III, *Confederate Edged Weapons.* Harper & Brothers, 1960.

Alexander, E. P., *Military Memoirs of a Confederate: A Critical Narrative.* Press of Morningside Bookshop, 1977.

The American Heritage Picture History of the Civil War. American Heritage Publishing Co., Inc., 1960.

Averell, William Woods, *Ten Years in the Saddle: The Memoir of William Woods Averell.* Presidio Press, 1978.

Barrett, Edwin S., *What I Saw at Bull Run: An Address.* Beacon Press, 1886.

Basler, Roy P., ed., *The Collected Works of Abraham Lincoln,* Vol. 4. Rutgers University Press, 1953.

Bates, Samuel P., *Martial Deeds of Pennsylvania.* T. H. Davis & Co., 1876.

Beatty, John, *Memoirs of a Volunteer, 1861-1863.* W. W. Norton & Co., Inc., 1946.

Blackford, W. W., *War Years with Jeb Stuart.* Charles Scribner's Sons, 1945.

Boatner, Mark Mayo, III, *The Civil War Dictionary.* David McKay Company, Inc., 1959.

Brock, R. A., ed., *Southern Historical Society Papers.* Kraus Reprint Co., 1977.

Butler, Benjamin F., *Butler's Book.* A. M. Thayer and Company, 1892.

Carnes, Eva Margaret, *The Tygarts Valley Line, June-July 1861.* First Land Battle of the Civil War Centennial Commemoration, Inc., 1961.

Carter, Robert Goldthwaite, *Four Brothers in Blue, or Sunshine and Shadows of the War of the Rebellion: A Story of the Great Civil War from Bull Run to Appomattox.* University of Texas Press, 1978.

Casler, John O., *Four Years in the Stonewall Brigade.* Press of Morningside Bookshop, 1981.

Catton, Bruce, *The Coming Fury (The Centennial History of the Civil War,* Vol. 1). Pocket Books, 1961.

Chase, Salmon P., *Inside Lincoln's Cabinet: The Civil War Diaries of Salmon P. Chase.* Longmans, Green, 1954.

Chittenden, Lucius E., *Invisible Siege: The Journal of Lucius E. Chittenden, April 15, 1861-July 14, 1861.* Americana Exchange Press, 1969.

Cooke, John Esten, *Wearing of the Gray: Being Personal Portraits, Scenes and Adventures of the War.* Kraus Reprint Co., 1977.

Cooling, Benjamin Franklin, *Symbol, Sword, and Shield.* Archon Books, 1975.

Cunliffe, Marcus, *Soldiers and Civilians: The Martial Spirit in America, 1775-1865.* Little, Brown and Company, 1968.

Curry, Richard Orr, *A House Divided: A Study of Statehood Politics and the Copperhead Movement in West Virginia.* University of Pittsburgh Press, 1964.

Davenport, Alfred, *Camp and Field Life of the Fifth New York Volunteer Infantry.* Dick and Fitzgerald, 1879.

Davis, George B., et al., *The Official Atlas of the Civil War.* Arno Press, 1978.

Davis, William C., *Battle at Bull Run: A History of the First Major Campaign of the Civil War.* Doubleday and Company, Inc., 1977.

Davis, William C., ed., *The Guns of '62 (The Image of War, 1861-1865,* Vol. 2). Doubleday and Company, Inc., 1982.

Dufour, Charles L., *Gentle Tiger: The Gallant Life of Roberdeau Wheat.* Louisiana State University Press, 1957.

Dyer, Frederick H., *A Compendium of the War of the Rebellion.* The National Historical Society in cooperation with the Press of Morningside Bookshop, 1979.

Early, Jubal Anderson, *War Memoirs: Autobiographical Sketch and Narrative of the War Between the States.* Indiana University Press, 1960.

Eaton, Clement, *Jefferson Davis.* Free Press, 1977.

Edwards, William B., *Civil War Guns.* Castle Books, 1962.

Elliott, Charles Winslow, *Winfield Scott: The Soldier and the Man.* Arno Press, 1979.

Elting, John R., *Long Endure: The Civil War Period, 1852-1867 (Military Uniforms in America,* Vol. 3). Presidio Press, 1982.

Esposito, Vincent J., ed., *The West Point Atlas of American Wars,* Vol. 1. Frederick A. Praeger, Publishers, 1959.

Fox, William F., *Regimental Losses in the American Civil War, 1861-1865.* Albany Publishing Company, 1893.

Freeman, Douglas Southall:
Manassas to Malvern Hill (Lee's Lieutenants: A Study in Command, Vol. 1). Scribner's, 1942.

R. E. Lee: A Biography, Vol. 1. Scribner's, 1934.

Fry, James B., *McDowell and Tyler in the Campaign of Bull Run.* D. Van Nostrand, 1884.

Fuller, Claud E., and Richard D. Steuart, *Firearms of the Confederacy.* Quarterman Publications, Inc., 1944.

Gibbon, John, *Personal Recollections of the Civil War.* Press of Morningside Bookshop, 1978.

Goss, Warren Lee, *Recollections of a Private: A Story of the Army of the Potomac.* Thomas Y. Crowell & Co., 1890.

Hanson, Joseph Mills, *Bull Run Remembers . . . The History, Traditions and Landmarks of the Manassas (Bull Run) Campaigns before Washington, 1861-1862.* National Capitol Publishers, Inc., 1961.

Hardee, W. J., *Rifle and Light Infantry Tactics; for the Exercise and Manoeuvres of Troops When Acting as Light Infantry or Riflemen.* J. B. Lippincott & Co., 1863.

Harris, William Charles, *Leroy Pope Walker: Confederate Secretary of War.* Confederate Pub. Co., 1962.

Hassler, Warren W., Jr.:
Commanders of the Army of the Potomac. Louisiana State University Press, 1962.
General George B. McClellan: Shield of the Union. Louisiana State University Press, 1957.

Heitman, Francis B., *Historical Register and Dictionary of the United States Army from Its Organization, September 29, 1789, to March 2, 1903.* University of Illinois Press, 1965.

Henderson, Lindsey P., Jr., *The Oglethorpe Light Infantry: A Military History.* The Civil War Centennial Commission of Savannah and Chatham County, 1961.

Hesseltine, William B., *Lincoln and the War Governors.* Alfred A. Knopf, 1955.

Holzman, Robert S., *Stormy Ben Butler.* Octagon Books, 1978.

Howard, McHenry, *Recollections of a Maryland Confederate Soldier and Staff Officer under Johnston, Jackson and Lee.* Press of Morningside Bookshop, 1975.

Ingraham, Charles A., *Elmer E. Ellsworth and the Zouaves of '61.* The University of Chicago Press, 1925.

Jackson, Mary Anna, *Memoirs of Stonewall Jackson.* The Prentice Press, 1895.

NEW FAIRFIELD FREE PUBLIC LIBRARY
NEW FAIRFIELD, CT.

Johannsen, Robert W., *Stephen A. Douglas*. Oxford University Press, 1973.

Johnson, Robert Underwood, and Clarence Clough Buel, eds., *Battles and Leaders of the Civil War*, Vol. 1. The Century Co., 1884-1887.

Jones, J. B., *A Rebel War Clerk's Diary at the Confederate States Capital*. Old Hickory Bookshop, 1935.

Kimball, William J., *Starve or Fall: Richmond and Its People, 1861-1865*. University Microfilms International, 1976.

Klein, Maury, *Edward Porter Alexander*. University of Georgia Press, 1971.

Lamers, William M., *The Edge of Glory: A Biography of General William S. Rosecrans, U.S.A.* Harcourt, Brace & World, Inc., 1961.

Lee, Richard M., *Mr. Lincoln's City: An Illustrated Guide to the Civil War Sites of Washington*. EPM Publications, Inc., 1981.

Leech, Margaret, *Reveille in Washington, 1860-1865*. Time-Life Books Inc., 1980.

Long, E. B., with Barbara Long, *The Civil War Day by Day*. Doubleday & Company, Inc., 1971.

Longstreet, James, *From Manassas to Appomattox: Memoirs of the Civil War in America*. Indiana University Press, 1981.

McClellan, George B., *McClellan's Own Story: The War for the Union*. Charles L. Webster & Company, 1887.

Michie, Peter S., *Great Commanders: General McClellan*. D. Appleton and Company, 1915.

Moore, Frank, ed., *The Civil War in Song and Story, 1860-1865*. P. F. Collier, Publisher, 1889.

Myers, Robert Manson, ed., *The Children of Pride: A True Story of Georgia and the Civil War*. Yale University Press, 1972.

Myers, William Starr, *A Study in Personality: General George Brinton McClellan*. D. Appleton-Century Company, 1934.

Naisawald, L. Van Loan, *Grape and Canister: The Story of the Field Artillery of the Army of the Potomac, 1861-1865*. Oxford University Press, 1960.

Nevins, Allan, *The Improvised War, 1861-1862 (The War for the Union*, Vol. 1). Charles Scribner's Sons, 1959.

Nunn, W. C., ed., *Ten Texans in Gray*. Hill Junior College Press, 1968.

Oates, Stephen B., *With Malice toward None: The Life of Abraham Lincoln*. Harper & Row, Publishers, 1977.

Official Records of the Union and Confederate Navies in the War of the Rebellion. Government Printing Office, 1896.

Owen, William Miller, *In Camp and Battle with the Washington Artillery of New Orleans*. Ticknor & Co., 1885.

Patrick, Rembert W., *Jefferson Davis and His Cabinet*. Louisiana State University Press, 1944.

Patterson, Robert, *A Narrative of the Campaign in the Valley of the Shenandoah in 1861*. Sherman & Co., Printers, 1865.

Personal Narratives of the Battles of the Rebellion. Sidney S. Rider, 1878.

Randall, J. G., *The Civil War and Reconstruction*. D. C. Heath and Company, 1937.

Randall, Ruth Painter, *Colonel Elmer Ellsworth: A Biography of Lincoln's Friend and First Hero of the Civil War*. Little, Brown and Company, 1960.

Reagan, John Henninger, *Memoirs, with Special Reference to Secession and the Civil War*. The Neale Publishing Company, 1906.

Richardson, H. Edward, *Cassius Marcellus Clay: Firebrand of Freedom*. University Press of Kentucky, 1976.

Robertson, James I., Jr., *The Stonewall Brigade*. Louisiana State University Press, 1963.

Robertson, James I., Jr., ed., *Proceedings of the Advisory Council of the State of Virginia, April 21-June 19, 1861*. Virginia State Library, 1977.

Roman, Alfred, *The Military Operations of General Beauregard in the War Between the States*. Harper & Brothers, 1883.

Russell, Sir William Howard, *My Diary North and South*. London: Bradbury and Evans, 1863.

Sandburg, Carl, *Abraham Lincoln: The War Years*. Harcourt, Brace & Company, 1939.

Shannon, Fred Albert, *The Organization and Administration of the Union Army, 1861-1865*. Peter Smith, 1965.

Smith, Elbert B., *Francis Preston Blair*. Free Press, 1930.

Smith, Merritt Roe, *Harpers Ferry Armory and the New Technology*. Cornell University Press, 1977.

Sprague, Dean, *Freedom under Lincoln* Houghton Mifflin, 1965.

Stampp, Kenneth M., *And the War Came*. Louisiana State University Press, 1980.

Staudenraus, P. J., ed., *Mr. Lincoln's Washington: Selections from the Writings of Noah Brooks, Civil War Correspondent*. Thomas Yoseloff, 1967.

Steffen, Randy, *The Frontier, the Mexican War, the Civil War, the Indian Wars, 1851-1880 (The Horse Soldier: 1776-1943*, Vol. 2). University of Oklahoma Press, 1978.

Strode, Hudson, *Jefferson Davis*. Harcourt, Brace, 1955-1964.

Strong, George Templeton, *Diary of the Civil War, 1860-1865*. Macmillan, 1962.

Thomas, Emory, *The Confederate Nation, 1861-1865*. Harper & Row, 1979.

Todd, Frederick P., *American Military Equipage, 1851-1872*. Charles Scribner's Sons, 1980.

Todd, William, *The Seventy-ninth Highlanders: New York Volunteers in the War of Rebellion, 1861-1865*. Press of Brandow, Barton & Co., 1886.

Townsend, Thomas S., *The Honors of the Empire State in the War of the Rebellion*. A. Lovell & Co., 1889.

U.S. Congress Joint Committee on the Conduct of the War, *The Battle of Bull Run*. Kraus Reprint Co., 1977.

The War of the Rebellion: A Compilation of the Official Records of the Union and Confederate Armies. Government Printing Office, 1880.

Warfield, Edgar, *A Confederate Soldier's Memoirs*. Masonic Home Press, Inc., 1936.

Warner, Ezra J.:
Generals in Blue: Lives of the Union Commanders. Louisiana State University Press, 1961.
Generals in Gray: Lives of the Confederate Commanders. Louisiana State University Press, 1959.

Wellman, Manly Wade, *Giant in Gray: A Biography of Wade Hampton of South Carolina*. Charles Scribner's Sons, 1949.

Wiley, Bell Irvin:
The Life of Billy Yank: The Common Soldier of the Union. Louisiana State University Press, 1981.
The Life of Johnny Reb: The Common Soldier of the Confederacy. Louisiana State University Press, 1980.

Williams, Kenneth P., *Lincoln Finds a General: A Military Study of the Civil War*. The Macmillan Company, 1949.

Williams, T. Harry:
Lincoln and His Generals. Vintage Books, 1952.
P.G.T. Beauregard: Napoleon in Gray. Louisiana State University Press, 1955.

Wilson, James Harrison, *Under the Old Flag*. Greenwood Press, 1971.

Woodsbury, Augustus, *The Second Rhode Island Regiment*. Providence, Valpey, Angell and Company, 1875.

Zinn, Jack, *The Battle of Rich Mountain*. Jack Zinn, 1971.

Other Sources

Ballou, Sullivan, letter to his wife. Civil War Letters Collection, Chicago Historical Society.

Bearss, Edwin C., "Troop Movement Maps: Battle of First Manassas and Engagement at Blackburn's Ford, July 18 & 21, 1861." *Historical Report on Troop Movements*, September 1981, Manassas National Battlefield Park, Virginia.

Boehm, Robert B., "Battle of Rich Mountain." *Civil War Times Illustrated*, February 1970.

Bradley, Chester D., "Controversial Ben Butler." *The Casemate Papers*, Fort Monroe Casemate Museum, Fort Monroe, Virginia.

Brown, Walter, Jr., ed., "More Terrible Than Victory: Benjamin Huske's Letter from Bethel." *Civil War Times Illustrated*, October 1981.

Gaines, Samuel M., letter dated December 24, 1902. Virginia Historical Society, Richmond, Virginia.

Gibbs, George Alphonso, "A Mississippi Private at First Bull Run and Ball's Bluff: An Eyewitness Account." *Civil War Times Illustrated*, April 1965.

Hall, James O., "Butler Takes Baltimore." *Civil War Times Illustrated*, August 1978.

"Highlights of Black History at Fort Monroe." *The Casemate Papers*, Fort Monroe Casemate Museum, Fort Monroe, Virginia.

Hundley, George A., "Beginning and the Ending: Reminiscences of the First and Last Days of the War." *Southern Historical Society Papers*, Vol. 23.

Hunter, Alexander, "Four Years in the Ranks." Unpublished ms., Virginia Historical Society, Richmond, Virginia.

"Is It a Fort or a Fortress?" *Tales of Old Fort Monroe*, Fort Monroe Casemate Museum, Fort Monroe, Virginia.

Jones, V. C., "First Manassas: The Story of the Bull Run Campaign." *Civil War Times Illustrated*, July 1980.

Keifer, J. Warren, "The Battle of Rich Mountain and Some Incidents." Paper read before the Ohio Commandery of the Loyal Legion, December 6, 1911.

Kimball, William J., "The Little Battle of Big Bethel." *Civil War Times Illustrated*, June 1967.

Luvaas, Jay, "An Appraisal of Joseph E. Johnston." *Civil War Times Illustrated*, January 1966.

McNeel, John A., "Famous Retreat from Philippi." *Southern Historical Society Papers*, 1906.

New York Leader, June 22, 1861.

The New York Times, June 18, 1861.

Patterson, Richard K., "Elmer Ellsworth: 'The Greatest Little Man . . .'" *American History Illustrated*, December 1971.

Peters, Winfield, "First Battle of Manassas." *Southern Historical Society Papers*, Vol. 34.

Thatcher, O. D., "The First Minnesota at Bull Run." *National Tribune*, June 3, 1886.

"Thirty-third Virginia at First Manassas." *Southern Historical Society Papers*, Vol. 34.

Thompson, Ai B., papers. Manassas National Battlefield Park, Virginia.

Wallace, Lee A., Jr., "Coppens' Louisiana Zouaves." *Civil War History*, September 1962.

Willcox, O. B., "Alexandria: Graphic Account of Its Capture and Occupation in 1861." *The National Tribune*, December 25, 1884.

Winthrop, Theodore, "New York Seventh Regiment: Our March to Washington." *The Atlantic Monthly*, June 1861.

PICTURE CREDITS

Credits from left to right are separated by semicolons, from top to bottom by dashes.

Cover: From *Battles of the Civil War*, the complete Kurz & Allison prints, published by Oxmoor House, Alabama. 2, 3: Map by Peter McGinn. 8, 9: New York State Historical Association, Cooperstown. 12, 13: Burton Historical Collection of the Detroit Public Library. 14, 15: Library of Congress. 16: Indianapolis Museum of Art, James E. Roberts Fund — from the collection of the Birmingham Museum of Art, gift of John E. Meyer, photographed by George Flemming. 17: The Peabody Museum of Salem, neg. no. 22,010. 18, 19: Library of Congress. 20, 21: The Western Reserve Historical Society. 22, 23: Courtesy Seventh Regiment Fund, Inc., photographed by Al Freni. 24, 25: Collections of the State Museum of Pennsylvania — the Meserve Collection of Mathew Brady negatives. National Portrait Gallery, Smithsonian Institution, Washington, D.C.; The Historical Society of Berks County, Reading, Pennsylvania, copied by Robert Walch. 26, 27: Courtesy of The New-York Historical Society — courtesy Gil Barrett. 28: Courtesy Seventh Regiment Fund, Inc., photographed by Al Freni. 30: The Western Reserve Historical Society. 32, 33: Courtesy of the New-York Historical Society. 34, 35: Vermont Historical Society. 36, 37: Courtesy of the Cincinnati Historical Society. 38, 39: Burton Historical Collection of the Detroit Public Library. 40, 41: Courtesy of the Rhode Island Historical Society, neg. no. RHI-X3-1692. 42, 43: Library of Congress. 45: Boston Public Library, Print Department. 47: Courtesy Jay P. Altmayer, photographed by Larry Cantrell; Military History Institute, Carlisle Barracks, Pennsylvania, copied by Robert Walch. 49: Military History Institute, Carlisle Barracks, Pennsylvania, copied by Robert Walch. 51: United States Military Academy Library, West Point, New York, copied by Al Freni — from *Rifle and Light Infantry Tactics*, published by J. B. Lippincott & Co., Philadelphia, 1863. 52, 53: Drawings by William J. Hennessy Jr. adapted from *Rifle and Light Infantry Tactics*, published by J. B. Lippincott & Co., Philadelphia, 1863. Photographs by Fil Hunter, courtesy Marine Corps Museum. 54: The Western Reserve Historical Society. 55: Courtesy William Gladstone. 58: Courtesy Herb Peck Jr. 59: Courtesy Seventh Regiment Fund, Inc., photographed by Al Freni. 60, 61: National Ar-

chives, neg. no. 111-B-4676. 62: The Meserve Collection of Mathew Brady negatives, National Portrait Gallery, Smithsonian Institution, Washington, D.C. 63: Chicago Historical Society, neg. no. 1980.227. 64: Virginia State Library — National Archives, neg. no. 165-SB-1. 65: Chicago Historical Society, neg. no. 1920.1038. 66, 67: Library of Congress; the Huntington Library, San Marino, California. 68, 69: The Meserve Collection of Mathew Brady negatives, National Portrait Gallery, Smithsonian Institution, Washington, D.C.; Division of Military & Naval Affairs (DMNA), State of New York, photographed by Henry Groskinsky — Chicago Historical Society (2) — courtesy Prince Gibson & Associates, Inc., Hudson, Ohio (2); the Harry T. Peters Collection, Museum of the City of New York. 70, 71: National Rifle Association, photographed by Leon Dishman — Fort Ward Museum, City of Alexandria, Virginia, photographed by Henry Beville — courtesy Harris Andrews, photographed by Fil Hunter — Fort Ward Museum, City of Alexandria, Virginia, photographed by Henry Beville. 72, 73: Fort Ward Museum, City of Alexandria, Virginia, photographed by Henry Beville. 74, 75: National Rifle Association, photographed by Leon Dishman. 77: Cairo Public Library, Cairo, Illinois. 78: Casemate Museum, Fort Monroe, Virginia, photographed by John Neubauer. 79: National Archives, neg. no. 111-B-4533. 81: Collection of Michael J. McAfee, courtesy Brian Pohanka. 82: Department of Archives and Manuscripts, Louisiana State University Library, Baton Rouge. 83: Confederate Imprints Collection, University of Georgia Library. 84, 85: Courtesy of The New-York Historical Society. 86: Atwater Kent Museum. 88: National Archives, neg. no. 111-B-4385. 89: West Virginia Department of Culture and History. 90: Courtesy of The New-York Historical Society. 91: Library of Congress. 92: West Virginia and Regional History Collection, West Virginia University Library. 94, 95: Library of Congress. 96, 97: The Western Reserve Historical Society. 98: From the Collection of Kean E. Wilcox. 99: The Museum of the Confederacy. 100: Courtesy C.D.W. Nelson. 101: Courtesy Jeffrey Brown. 102: Courtesy L. M. Strayer. 103: The Museum of the Confederacy. 104: Valentine Museum. 105: Courtesy Herb Peck Jr. 106: Courtesy Jeffrey Brown. 107: Courtesy Herb Peck Jr. 108: Military History Institute, Carlisle Barracks, Pennsylvania, copied by Robert Walch. 109: South Carolin-

iana Library, University of South Carolina. 112: Library of Congress. 114, 115: Courtesy of the Boston Athenaeum. 116: National Archives, neg. no. 111-B-4448. 119, 120: Military History Institute, Carlisle Barracks, Pennsylvania, copied by Robert Walch. 121: Virginia Historical Society, photographed by George Nan. 123: Library of Congress. 124: National Park Service. 125: The Washington Light Infantry of Charleston, South Carolina, photographed by Harold H. Norvell; Arkansas Commemorative Commission, Old State House Museum — the Confederate Memorial Hall, New Orleans, Louisiana, photographed by John R. Miller; the Museum of the Confederacy, photographed by Henry Beville — Virginia Military Institute Museum, photographed by Henry Beville; Smyth County Historical and Museum Society Inc., Marion, Virginia, photographed by Eddie Le Sueur. 126: Courtesy H. Armstrong Roberts, Inc. 127: Library of Congress. 128: Map by Walter Roberts. 129: Valentine Museum. 130, 131: Library of Congress. 132: South Caroliniana Library, University of South Carolina. 133: Map by Walter Roberts. 134: Library of Congress. 137: Division of Military & Naval Affairs (DMNA), State of New York, photographed by Henry Groskinsky. 138: Courtesy Brian Pohanka. 139: South Caroliniana Library, University of South Carolina. 140: From *Battles and Leaders of the Civil War*, Vol. 1, published by the Century Company, 1884-1887. 141: Map by Walter Roberts. 142: Library of Congress — from *Battles and Leaders of the Civil War*, Vol. 1, published by the Century Company, 1884-1887. 144: Library of Congress. 146: Map by Walter Roberts. 148: Library of Congress. 149: The Museum of the Confederacy, photographed by Henry Beville. 150, 151: National Archives, neg. no. 111-B-5148. 152: From the Collections of the Louisiana State Museum. 153, 154: Library of Congress. 156, 157: McLellan Lincoln Collection, John Hay Library, Brown University. 158, 159: Courtesy Frank W. Wood, inset Library of Congress. 160, 161: From *Deeds of Valor*, Vol. 1, published by the Perrien-Keydel Company, Detroit, Michigan, 1906. 162, 163: Courtesy Sidney King. 164-165: Courtesy Dr. Larry Freeman, American Life Foundation, Watkins Glen, New York, photographed by Lon Mattoon. 166, 167: The Confederate Memorial Hall, New Orleans, Louisiana. 168, 169: United States Naval Academy Beverley R. Robinson Collection.

INDEX

NEW FAIRFIELD FREE PUBLIC
LIBRARY
NEW FAIRFIELD, CT.

NEW FAIRFIELD FREE PUBLIC LIBRARY NEW FAIRFIELD, CT.